HOW TO ACCOMPANY AT THE PIANO

HOW TO ACCOMPANY AT THE PIANO

1. PLAIN ACCOMPANIMENT
2. FIGURATED ACCOMPANIMENT
3. PRACTICAL HARMONY FOR ACCOMPANISTS

BY
EDWIN EVANS, SENIOR, F R.C.O.

172 MUSIC EXAMPLES
Which are made clear by the Explanatory Text

**Fredonia Books
Amsterdam, The Netherlands**

How to Accompany at the Piano

by
Edwin Evans

ISBN: 1-58963-656-2

Copyright © 2001 by Fredonia Books

Fredonia Books
Amsterdam, The Netherlands
http://www.fredoniabooks.com

All rights reserved, including the right to reproduce this book, or portions thereof, in any form.

In order to make original editions of historical works available to scholars at an economical price, this facsimile of the original edition is reproduced from the best available copy and has been digitally enhanced to improve legibility, but the text remains unaltered to retain historical authenticity.

PREFACE.

THE object of this little book is to assist those who desire to excel in the art of accompaniment and are equipped with a sufficient musical knowledge upon which to base the necessary explanations. The subject is therefore approached as one entirely apart from ordinary playing, the reader's attention being concentrated upon various styles of accompaniment in such a way as to yield instruction in mode of performance from the general conformation of the accompaniments themselves

The classifications required in course of this project have naturally led to a profuse number of examples, the full signification of which it may be hoped is made clear by the explanatory text; and, in order to extend the use of each example beyond the case to which it is immediately applied, special stress has been laid upon the subjects of figuration and of harmony (in its more practical phase). To each of these a separate section of the book has been devoted.

Preface.

The treatment of modulation and transposition from the accompanist's point of view has incidentally led to some elucidations possessing an even wider field of interest; as, for example, in the scheme of universal modulation by the diminished seventh chord (Ex. 160) and in many other cases which might be mentioned This, however, is no more than is natural to expect; for the same musicianship which favours a good accompanist cannot fail to lend itself to more extended application. Our present compulsion to be *practical before all things* confers therefore upon the subject of accompaniment a special value for the ordinary musical reader.

EDWIN EVANS, SENIOR.

LONDON, *1917.*

CONTENTS.

	PAGE.
PREFACE	v
CONTENTS	vii

PART I.
PRACTICAL ACCOUNT OF THE VARIOUS FORMS OF PLAIN ACCOMPANIMENT.

CHAPTER I.
GENERAL SURVEY OF THE SUBJECT ... 3

CHAPTER II.
ON DIFFERENT STYLES OF UNISON ACCOMPANIMENT ... 17

CHAPTER III.
ON SUSTAINED HARMONIES IN ACCOMPANIMENT ... 25

CHAPTER IV.
ACCOMPANIMENT BY SIMPLE HARMONISATION ... 35

CHAPTER V.
ON VARIOUS USES OF THE HOLDING-NOTE IN ACCOMPANIMENT ... 44

CHAPTER VI.
ON ACCOMPANIMENT WITH THE MELODY AS BASS OR INNER PART ... 55

CHAPTER VII.
ON POLYPHONIC ACCOMPANIMENT ... 65

PART II.
FIGURED ACCOMPANIMENT.

CHAPTER VIII.
ON THE MAJOR TRIAD AS BASIS FOR FIGURATION ... 73

CHAPTER IX.
ACCOMPANIMENTS FORMED BY TRIPLET DISPERSIONS OF THE TRIAD ... 82

Contents.

CHAPTER X.
Accompaniments Formed from Further Triad Dispersions ... 93

CHAPTER XI.
Accompaniments Formed from Broken Chords ... 102

CHAPTER XII.
Rhythmical Figures of Accompaniment ... 112

CHAPTER XIII.
Alternated Hand-Motion in Accompaniment ... 122

CHAPTER XIV.
Ostinato Figures of Accompaniment (Rhythmical) ... 130

CHAPTER XV.
Ostinato Figures of Accompaniment (Characteristic) ... 137

PART III.
PRACTICAL HARMONY FOR ACCOMPANISTS.

CHAPTER XVI.
On the Minor Triad in Accompaniment ... 149

CHAPTER XVII.
Triad Positions Required in Accompaniment ... 164

CHAPTER XVIII.
Tetrad Positions Required in Accompaniment ... 170

CHAPTER XIX.
The Dominant Seventh in Modulation ... 178

CHAPTER XX.
The Diminished Seventh in Modulation ... 193

CHAPTER XXI.
Chromatic Modulation ... 202

CHAPTER XXII
Transposition ... 211

Conclusion ... 217

GENERAL INDEX ... 221

PART I

PRACTICAL ACCOUNT
of the Various Forms of
PLAIN ACCOMPANIMENT

CHAPTER I.

GENERAL SURVEY OF THE SUBJECT.

1. At what particular stage in the player's training does accompaniment appeal to him as a separate subject?

To ask this question is practically to fix the class of reader to whom this book is to be addressed; for, in the case of a very moderate executant, to play and to accompany is all one. While we are troubled with mechanics we cannot possibly subordinate our will to the intentions of another performer; besides which, even when we begin to conquer such difficulties, we have still to await some knowledge of phrasing and the consequent practice in graduations of touch.

Then it is that we begin to notice the separate treatment due to subordinate parts, and that is the stage of progress to be looked upon as qualifying the reader to enter upon the study of accompaniment as it is described in these pages.

2. When once this interest in the relative importance of parts has been awakened it becomes natural to us to take pleasure in performance, either with some other

one instrument or in chamber pieces; such as trios, and the like. All this is well; though it would be a great mistake to suppose it to constitute the entire art of pianoforte accompaniment. A vast distinction lies between vocal and instrumental rendering; for the reason that the voice stands alone in music as the association of articulate with tonal sound. This means that the musical phrase, instead of being something bearing only an ethereal and mysterious meaning, is now wedded to the fixed and positive ideas of our ordinary speech; and that the medium by which those ideas reach us must necessarily be the one upon which our attention is to be concentrated, no matter what others may be employed to contribute to the general effect. In thus deriving our principal interest from the text we assume, to some extent, the same position as the composer; who draws his inspiration from the same source.

3. These facts, though merely elementary, are of extreme importance, as furnishing us with a reliable starting point for our inquiry. By means of them we see at once that, in the preliminary stage, the voice does not require accompaniment at all; and that the unaccompanied folk-song may, from one point of view, be regarded as more ideal than when it is subjected to an artistic setting. This being so, the primitive purpose of accompaniment can only have been to support the voice; which is equivalent to stating that its most natural form is that in which it simply joins the voice,

either in octave or in unison. Such, in fact, was the only kind of accompaniment once even possible; it is one still largely used with noble effect in church music; and it is also one to which great composers still resort when the sentiment to be expressed is sufficiently solemn, religious, earnest or bold to require it (Ex. 1).

Ex. 1.

4. The next style of accompaniment is that which consists of a plain harmonisation of the melody, and is one which combines support of the voice with harmonic colour. It assumes the separate harmonisation of each

note, and is therefore best applied to airs which proceed by even steps of time-duration. The melody again appears as the upper note of each chord, thus affording the same kind of support as that of the first style; the distinction from which consists alone in the harmonic background which has been added (Ex. 2).

Ex. 2.

5 If, now, we remove the melody from this form of accompaniment and allow the latter to consist of the harmonic background only, we evolve a third style; in which support for the voice is no longer derived from

any kind of contact upon the level but entirely from a harmonic foundation. Change of effect results from this procedure, as the vocal part becomes more salient by being free; in addition to which the harmony becomes more discernible as a background by being separated (Ex. 3).

6. But, all this time, we have been principally contemplating the treatment of airs consisting of notes of equal value; which is a description confined to the chorale and to the simplest types of folk-song. In other words, it relates to a serious and earnest feeling which is only one of various shades of sentiment; each of which has, at one time or other, to be expressed. Various moods call for different rhythms, and these consist of tone-successions made up of notes of differing time-value. Some notes will accordingly be short; and, for these, the voice can neither require support nor can it be necessary to supply such unimportant notes with any special background of harmony. In the fourth style we shall therefore find some notes re-

maining unaccompanied; whilst the same chord will very likely sustain during the vocal performance of several successive notes; this generally coinciding with some division, either in the sense of the words or in the rhythm. In the following pages this kind of sustained accompaniment is described as consisting of the "phrase-chord"; under which heading the reader will find the matter copiously treated (Ex. 4).

7. We are therefore at present free to pass on to the fifth style of accompaniment, or that which establishes a minimum rhythmic pulsation for the whole piece. Thus, supposing a song to be in common time, the minimum rhythmic pulsation will probably be the quaver; and, although notes of this value may only be found occasionally in the voice part, they will be liable to occur at any time in the accompaniment; as a means of sustaining the rhythmic motion during a vocal sostenuto, or whenever, for various other reasons, this measuring-out of the rhythmic pulsation may appear

General Survey of the Subject.

desirable. Such a style of accompaniment is precisely the reverse of that of the "phrase-chord"; in which the rhythmic pulsation is stilled, or, as it were, brought to rest. Yet, in its first stage, it partakes of the same simple nature; for it contemplates nothing beyond the plainest harmonisation, and, in working, consists merely of repeated chords; under which heading it is treated in the following pages, so that nothing more with regard to it need now be said (Ex. 5).

8. Observation of the example will show that, while chord repetition undoubtedly furnishes the required pulsation, it is inclined to be somewhat cumbrous; and that the harmonic sensation of the chord, as well as the rhythmic pulsation, might have been equally obtained by taking the notes in succession; or, in arpeggio, as it is called. This distribution of the notes of the harmony is the basis of what is called figuration, and is so important a matter that one complete section of this work will be devoted to it. It would be impossible to estimate, even approximately, the number of types of accompaniment to which it gives rise; but, as they all originate from the same source, and as we are at present merely considering the matter in a broad sense, the most elementary figuration possible is presented as typical of a sixth style (Ex. 6).

Ex. 6.

9 As the style last mentioned comprises within itself every ornamental design which can possibly be invented, the remaining types of accompaniment may be very shortly summarised. As seventh in order may be mentioned the transfer of the melody to the bass of the accompaniment (as also occasionally to an inner part) producing various effects to be described hereafter (Ex. 7); and with this the essentials of accom-

Ex. 7.

paniment may be said to conclude. Such refinements as we have so far encountered originate merely in the rhythm and plain harmonisation of the melody. Even the grand resource of figuration, notwithstanding its myriad forms, does not necessarily draw upon the higher resources of harmony As for counterpoint, if the name can be invoked at all, it can only be said to consist of two parts—the melody and its bass; whilst both form and rhythm have been simply that of the air Thus, comprehensive as the list may seem to some readers to be, the journey we have taken so far has only brought us to the threshold of the really artistic department of the subject.

10 The resources of harmony are so immense that it would be an injustice to the subject to do more than allude in this place to their inestimable value; but we may select the feature of the *holding note* to represent them for the moment, in the same way that we selected the *simple arpeggio* as a type of figuration (Ex. 8)

General Survey of the Subject

11 The same may be said of rhythm in its multitudinous applications for purposes of accompaniment; the instance selected to do duty in our present rapid survey being one of *counter-melody* leading to an extension of the phrase (Ex. 9).

12 Then as the result of a special application of counterpoint, we have the polyphonic style of accompaniment, either with or without allowing the melody to appear as one of the voices; a short sample of the latter of which is given in Ex. 10.

Ex. 10.

General Survey of the Subject. 15

13 And, lastly, there is that masterly style of accompaniment in which not only all the resources hitherto mentioned are freely drawn upon, but which dictates the form of the composition itself; by having recourse to orchestral motives in illustration of the text, by counter-melodies, *obbligato* basses, interspersed symphonies and the like. Of this type it is obviously impossible to give an example without doing so *in extenso* We shall therefore characterise it as "concertante" accompaniment; concluding our epitome by

referring the reader to the tabular exposition of the contents of this chapter (Ex 11).

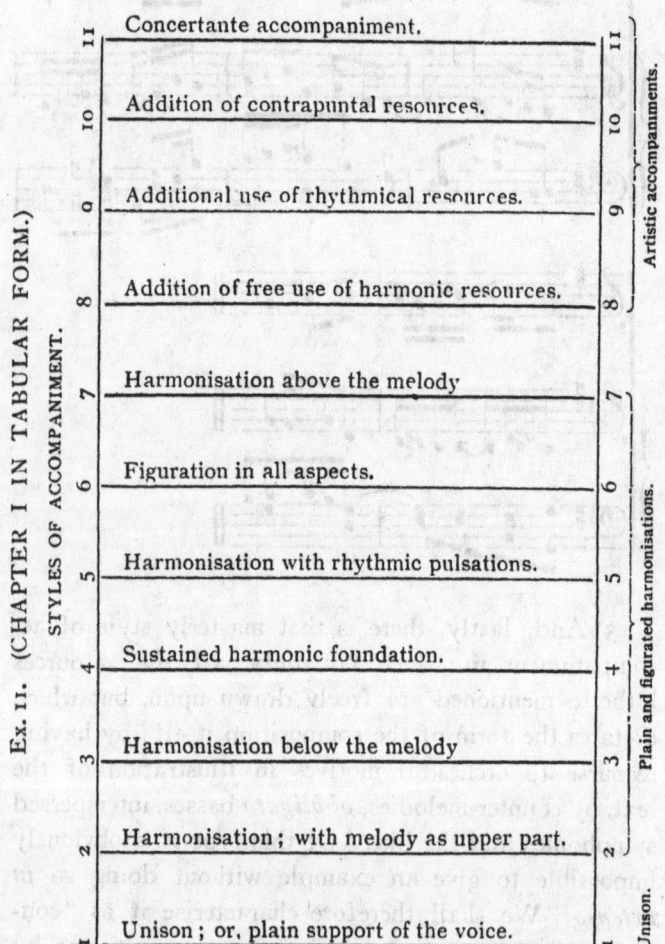

Ex. 11. (CHAPTER I IN TABULAR FORM.) STYLES OF ACCOMPANIMENT.

11	Concertante accompaniment.	11 ⎫
10	Addition of contrapuntal resources.	10 ⎬ Artistic accompaniments.
9	Additional use of rhythmical resources.	9
8	Addition of free use of harmonic resources.	8 ⎭
7	Harmonisation above the melody	7 ⎫
6	Figuration in all aspects.	6
5	Harmonisation with rhythmic pulsations.	5 ⎬ Plain and figurated harmonisations.
4	Sustained harmonic foundation.	4
3	Harmonisation below the melody	3
2	Harmonisation; with melody as upper part.	2 ⎭
1	Unison; or, plain support of the voice.	1 Unison.

CHAPTER II

ON DIFFERENT STYLES OF UNISON ACCOMPANIMENT

14 ALL the various styles of accompaniment detailed in the last chapter exist, more or less, in solo music for the instrument; but it is impossible for them to attain the same development when the hands have to provide both melody and accompaniment as when the sole care is to assist an already existing melody. The consequence is that the figurations used in accompaniment are partly more elaborate—but partly, also, of a different kind altogether from those used in solo performance; and the student's first care should be to master all the leading types. He will find it much easier to do this by the aid of knowledge of the subject, than by any form of practice, consisting merely of repetitions; and the plan now to be pursued will consist, therefore, of precept and explanation.

15. In the tabular view given in Ex. 11 figuration appears, unavoidably, as merely *one* means of accompaniment; but the reader must not thereby be induced to confound it with the others, to which it bears not

the slightest resemblance. When we speak of melody, harmony or rhythm, we speak of musical *material*; but figuration is only a *treatment* of material already provided. Even accompaniment in the unison, as we shall presently see, may be figured; in short, figuration applies to everything. Thus, the same material may be figured either rhythmically, melodically or harmonically; and the great art of the accompanist, so far as mere execution is concerned, is to trace, *quickly*, the simple material which underlies the complex passages he may encounter.

This must be thoroughly well understood before the reader can proceed to consider the various styles of accompaniment in detail; and, whatever they may be, they are *all* subject to figuration.

16. First comes the "unison" style, in plain form; which, notwithstanding its elementary nature, is not quite easy to play, with absolute precision. Even fair average players have a common habit of unconsciously allowing the two hands to take the notes forming the octave slightly *after* one another, commencing with the left hand An instance of this defect is shown in Ex. 12; and occasion may be taken to mention that, in pianoforte accompaniment, apparent simplicity of execution is always dangerous to the careless player Correct phrasing is important at all times, but doubly so in simple passages; because there is then no detail to help it, and everything depends upon touch. Take, for instance, the passage given at Ex. 13, in which

Different Styles of Unison Accompaniment.   19

Ex. 12.

the phrase may be easily rendered "angular" by bad accompaniment. A word of warning may also be helpful not to rely too much upon legato signs as indicative of the phrasing; on account of the twofold use to which the slur is applied. In Ex. 13, for instance,

Ex. 13.

the slurs are those published; but the slur in dotted line shows the *real* extent of the last phrase. The reader will perceive that the expression is despondent.

How to Accompany.

This, to a skilful accompanist, would imply a shade of *diminuendo* in each case; whereas, had the expression been exultant, the reverse would have happened.

17. The next phase of unison accompaniment is that in which it is practically, but not absolutely identical with the voice part. In this variety refinement of touch is again most desirable, for additional reasons. Thus, the trifling divergencies between piano and voice may be of a nature to require the individuality of the piano

Different Styles of Unison Accompaniment. 21

to be almost extinguished at certain points. A sample of this kind of thing is presented by Ex. 14 *(a)*, in which, at the places marked *(a)*, the small notes only exist for the production of a quasi-portamento effect, similar to the gliding of the voice, or violin glissando; whilst at those marked *(b)* the voice suspends the note,

Ex 14. *(b)*.

momentarily, by a semitone with the result of imposing a *pp* upon the accompaniment for obvious reasons.

18. We now come to figurations of the unison, which are necessarily not so varied as those of full chords; though it must not be supposed that, in consequence of harmony being absent, there can be no harmonic inflections. As rhythmical inflections begin with dispersion between the two hands, whereby the effect and assistance of the unison is retained without covering the voice, it follows that the majority of such accompaniments are played very staccato; besides which, it is a common feature to find the unison still further

disguised by being mingled with fragments of harmony. A good accompanist should at once see that the intention in such cases is to assist the vocal intonation in commencing the phrase. A simple instance of this is given by Ex. 15.

19. The reader is sure to meet with beautiful designs worked from this simple expedient, and, whenever he does so (in default of express reason to the contrary) it is his duty to subside after assisting the

Ex. 15.

Different Styles of Unison Accompaniment. 23

voice to the phrase-commencement. A very useful instance is presented by Ex. 15, as, in this case, the assistance rendered by the accompaniment recurs quickly again and again.

20. We now come to what appears at first sight to be almost a contradiction in terms; namely, the unison accompaniment with harmonic inflections. A figure of this kind enables the player very greatly to assist the voice without appearing to do so; which partly arises from the fact that the accompaniment is really in the

Ex 16

unison without appearing to be so. But, in order to secure these advantages, some adroit graduations of touch are necessary, as may be gathered from Ex. 16. Here the arpeggio figure of the right-hand part gives the effect of a harmonised accompaniment, notwithstanding that the voice is continually assisted in the unison, by one or other of the two hands.

CHAPTER III.

ON SUSTAINED HARMONIES IN ACCOMPANIMENT.

21. NEXT to unison accompaniment in point of simplicity of material comes the "phrase-chord"; or, single harmony adjusted to more or less of the vocal part, according to how far the melodic inflections of the latter render this possible. The piano's want of sostenuto power prevents the phrase-chord being used for very long in simple form; though it is liable to occur in tremolo, this being the best (as it is also the most familiar) means of imitating a sustained chord. An instance of its use for the prolongation of a phrase-chord is given by Ex. 17, at the right hand line marked (a). There, it will be seen that, first the chord of B flat, and afterwards that of F dominant is sustained for three bars. At (b) the same sostenuto is effected by arpeggio; and, at (c), we have the plain chords. The reader will perceive, therefore, that the material of these three accompaniments is precisely the same, the expression of (a), (b) and (c) being respectively agitated, blithe and placidly harmonious

26 *How to Accompany.*

Ex 17

On Sustained Harmonies in Accompaniment. 27

22. So prolonged a use of the phrase-chord is useful here for purposes of illustration; but it is rare in modern music to find the voice-part so long amenable to one harmony. In practice we should generally find such extensions associated with an interspersed symphony, and this latter possessed of some meaning in connection with the text. The treatment would of course depend upon the idea to be expressed; but, in the majority of cases, there would be a slight *crescendo* for the symphony, after which the accompaniment would subside for the next vocal entry. A case of this kind is presented in Ex. 18, and will serve also

How to Accompany

Ex. 18.

to show, incidentally, how desirable it is for an accompanist to cultivate a light tremolo. As the idea to be presented is one of even continuity, it follows that there should be no accentuation, though frequent instances occur in which a sudden *sforzando* is required. This effect, which is highly orchestral and dramatic, should be produced if possible with the unaided finger; and the unseemly thrust, so common with indifferent accompanists, avoided.

On Sustained Harmonies in Accompaniment. 29

23. It may occasionally happen that a chord is written to be sustained for a longer time than the tone of the instrument endures; not from any fault of the composer, but probably on account of the accompaniment having been arranged from the band score Cases of this kind call for some exercise of judgment on the part of the accompanist; who, by studying the

Ex 19

rhythm, will always be able to discover some spot at which the tone may be gently renewed without injury to the general effect. Above all things he should not play the chord *louder*, in order that the sound may endure; as this would be a greater evil than letting it die away before the time; and there is no excuse for such a proceeding, as a good accompanist can always (and especially during a vocal phrase of any animation) renew the chord without anyone being aware of his having done so. This is a matter best studied by every player for himself.

24. Having thus disposed of what may be called extreme cases, we have now to deal with the common use of the phrase-chord, an instance of which is given in Ex 19 The effect is generally soft; because, if the sentiment to be expressed were not restful, the harmony would not be sustained. Thus, where the

accompaniment is designed to be assertive, it is generally associated with a changeful harmony. The mere fact of one chord being retained, even although the composer may not wish it to be sustained, is also, in most cases, equivalent to a *piano*; as in the two short examples, 20 and 21.

25. When the phrase-chord is only slightly sustained the accompanist must carefully observe the voice-part, as melodic inflections are liable to introduce notes outside the chord; and this also implies a hushed

effect, for obvious reasons. An instance is given with Ex. 22.

26. It may be observed that the whole of the foregoing relates to the use of sostenuto chords during changes in the voice-part; but it is clear that the reasons for the advice given to the player in favour of soft effects will be reversed in the opposite case; or, that is to say, when it is the *voice* which remains stationary and the *harmony* which changes. By re-

maining stationary, however, a mere repetition of the same note is not to be understood; because this would imply that the rhythm is not by any means stationary—and, in practice, it is on such occasions mostly rather quickened and agitated. A sample of this is given with Ex. 23; which, for the reason stated, is a soft effect.

27. But when the voice, instead of repeating its note, sustains it, and when, during its continuance,

On Sustained Harmonies in Accompaniment. 33

the chord of the accompaniment changes, the case is altogether different. Never does the effect of an accompaniment appear to greater advantage. For the moment, the effect of the ensemble is then in the player's keeping; and (with due regard to the sentiment of the piece) he should take care to make the new harmony thoroughly well felt. An illustration of this is presented by Ex. 24.

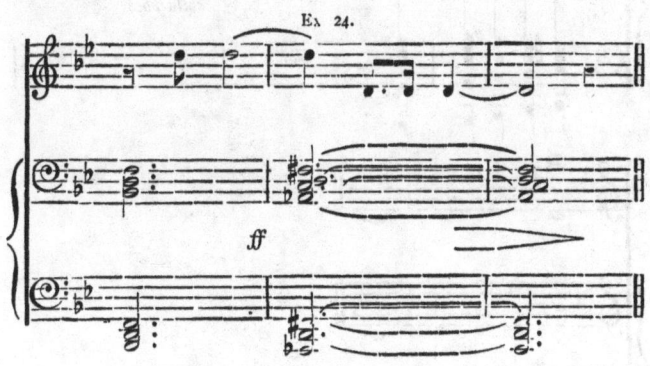

Ex. 24.

28. It will be noticed that in this example the voice sustains and swells out to a powerful accent, which is an essential of the case in view. Sometimes the harmony may even change several times during the vocal sostenuto, in which case there will be a *crescendo* during the whole time. But, should the voice change its note when the accent arrives, the passage is no longer the same; or, should the changes in the harmony merely consist of modifications of the same

chord, the foregoing does not apply. Each of these typical situations will be made clear by Ex. 25, at

the points marked *(a)* and *(b)* respectively. The phrase-chord may now be considered sufficiently explained for practical purposes.

CHAPTER IV

ACCOMPANIMENT BY SIMPLE HARMONISATION.

29 THE plain harmonisation of a melody presents its simplest appearance when the notes are of equal value; but its nature remains the same whatever may be the rhythm of the theme, providing a separate chord be allotted for each note, and providing, also, that the melody remains in the upper part. The principal difficulty of this kind of accompaniment arises from the temptation to treat it negligently; for, the only object of the upper notes being to assist the voice, a slight difference of touch is desirable for them; and the habit of this is by no means easy to acquire. It is easy enough to make a *great* difference, but that is not wanted. On the contrary, the skilful accompanist will restrict even the slight preference in amount of tone given to the upper notes to the strong beats of the bar; unless, of course, the voice should require more continued assistance, in which case he must be ready to render it. A passage accompanied in this way is shown in Ex. 26.

Ex. 26.

30. Melodies accompanied thus plainly are generally themselves of simple character; and the first sign of the composer desiring the voice to be free consists of his allowing the plain harmonisation to be only a background, as in Ex. 3; or, as might have been effected by simply leaving out the upper notes of the accompaniment in Ex. 26. For a special illustration, however, the reader is referred to the treatment shown in Ex. 27.

31. This kind of accompaniment has the advantage of being very full, and frequently requires subduing on that account. The accompanist should therefore accustom himself to the touch required for playing large chords with a soft effect, as he will frequently be called upon for this In Ex. 26, for instance, octaves might easily have been added, without the accompaniment being desired to be any louder; and the special touch required for this is one in which the fin-

Accompaniment by Simple Harmonisation

Ex. 27.

gers merely allow the keys sufficient room to rise, so that the next blow becomes one of mere pressure from the key-surface. A special instance is provided by Ex. 28.

32. So long as the accompaniment follows the rhythm of the melody in detail (which is the case with all the foregoing examples) it amounts to a plain harmonisation, the first departure from which usually

takes the form of a separate rhythmic figure. It is the business of the accompanist to take note of this figure at once, as it is extremely likely to permeate

E. 28.

the whole composition This, however, only renders it the more easy to trace; and, generally speaking, a mere glance at the aspect of the notation is sufficient to reveal it. Such figures, in their most elementary form, constitute scarcely any change from a simple

Accompaniment by Simple Harmonisation. 39

harmonisation; their importance lying in the fact that they give a special rhythmical impress to the entire composition; and, whether the effect be loud or soft, they must be reproduced relatively with the same graduations of touch. A sample figure of this description is presented by Ex. 29; from which it will be

Ex. 29.

perceived that the smoothness of passing from first to second beat, and the extreme lightness of the latter are the only features which distinguish this accompaniment from that of Ex 26, except that the importance and usefulness of such a feature appears by its repetition after each line of the text. The employment of this figure does not cease during the whole song in which it occurs, which will give the reader some idea of the importance of the matter—this being by no means an exceptional case.

33. We have naturally selected one of the simplest examples by way of elucidating this matter in the first instance; and we will now pass on to a case in which,

Ex 30

Accompaniment by Simple Harmonisation. 41

while the harmony remains equally plain, a separate rhythmical figure is allotted to the bass. Bass figures are in great request on account of their presenting great musical interest without impeding the voice; but they require a crisp touch, and, it need scarcely be said, a complete abstention from use of the damper pedal. Ex. 30 will illustrate all this; and, at the same time, exhibit the minimum rhythmic pulsations which were spoken of in Chapter I, in connection with Ex. 5, and which will hereafter be specially dealt with under the head of "chord repetitions."

34. Accompaniments such as that of Ex. 30 are rarely played well, because of lack of independence between the two hands. Obviously the right hand part should sympathise with the melody; instead of which the majority of players, by adjusting it to the bass, mark the second beat too strongly. The object of mentioning this is to point out that bass figures in accompaniment should be played as independently as if they were being performed by a separate instrument. This however only applies to cases in which they have a distinct character, and has nothing to do with bass figures which are entirely subordinate to the main rhythm, as in Ex. 31.

35. Mention was made in connection with Ex. 30 of chord-repetition which, though combined with plainly harmonised accompaniment, is reserved for separate treatment. The same may be said of hand-alternation, an example of which will now be given

Ex. 31

in the same way. An observation of Ex. 32 will show that it is really a plain harmonisation, notwithstanding the light character imparted to it by the alternation. The same might also be said of "figurations"; which form a separate study in themselves, but which apply to every kind of material, as was explained at the opening of Chapter II. If the rhythmic figure has been admitted to this chapter, therefore, it has only

Ex. 32

Accompaniment by Simple Harmonisation

been by way of showing how naturally plain harmonisation allies itself with the higher features of accompaniment.

CHAPTER V.

ON VARIOUS USES OF THE HOLDING-NOTE IN ACCOMPANIMENT.

36. THE accompanist is so frequently called upon to work effects from notes which being common to succeeding harmonies form connecting links between them that, after plain harmonisation, his first attention is due to this subject. Such effects are indeed utilised in almost every vocal composition; their most familiar form being the "holding-note," or note sustained over a change of chord. The prime object of the composer being to produce a smooth effect we may expect the use of such notes to be most frequent in the extreme parts, where they are naturally capable of exerting a more binding influence. The object of their presence being so clear, the obligation of the accompanist to render them prominently is equally so; though the measure of this prominence will of course depend upon the idea which is being expressed. The most usual case of holding-note is that in which the dominant is retained as fifth in the tonic chord; and

vice versa. A sample of this is shown in Ex 33,

where it will be observed that at *(a)* the G of the upper part remains a constant feature at the change of chord. The reader can scarcely fail to be already familiar with this use made of the fifth of every key, and we may therefore immediately pass on to refer to its varied expression. In the example just quoted the idea is that of a lullaby, but this is only one out of a great number of suitable applications, the discussion of which would lead us away from the strictly musical subject Sometimes the retention of the one note takes the form of reiteration, as in Ex. 34, the performance remaining placid in the absence of special feature in the vocal part, but sympathising by *crescendo* with any important rise or sostenuto, as at the point marked *(a)*. The amount of tone to be given to such notes will generally depend upon their relation in point of length to the rest of the accompaniment Thus in Ex. 33 they were longer and would therefore be louder than the rest; whilst in Ex. 34 the

opposite is the case. Independently of the lighter motion, which alone would suggest a softer touch in the last case, there is the fact that the repeated note often occurs by itself, and therefore requires no emphasis to make itself heard

37. In addition to such cases there is of course that in which the repeated notes are of equal duration to

the remainder. The distinction is then of the slightest and may be described as a tenuto of the upper note, as in Ex. 35.

38. But there are also occasions when even this faint prominence is not required, and when the mere presence of the holding-note as a connecting link is sufficient to produce the desired effect. This will occur when all the notes of the accompaniment without dis-

tinction are of equal length, and it is rarer to hear this played with perfect evenness of weight than to find prominence correctly given; especially when the latter takes place at either extremity of the hand, from which point it is easy for the hand-weight to give support. A sample of this kind of passage is given with Ex. 36; and in executing it much benefit will be experienced by using the finger elasticity in aid of

Ex. 36.

On Various Uses of the Holding-Note.

the wrist. The effect here intended is that of the distant horn, and occasion may be taken to mention the similar application of the holding-note to fanfare effects of all descriptions.

39 In the next example the holding-note is used for the purpose of giving prominence to an effect which is purely rhythmical, viz, the measured tread of a wayfarer. The quaver motion would have given this to a certain extent unaided; but without an even top-surface the occasional sway of a person walking could not have been so correctly given as at the temporary deviations marked *(a)* and *(b)* Ex. 37. The accom-

panist will do well to *crescendo* slightly for the moment, subsiding to *pp* as soon as the holding-note is resumed. It is usual to give some relief to the monotony of the holding-note in this way; and when, as in this case, a poetical reason exists, this takes place during the vocal phrase. But, otherwise, it is liable to occur in the accompaniment alone and in completion of the phrase, as in Ex. 38; forming in this way a

Ex. 38.

slight introduction to "concertante" accompaniment as mentioned in Chapter I, and in which, in addition to fulfilling the duties of strict accompaniment, the instrumental part contributes to the main outline of the piece. In this example the object of the holding-note is distinctly rhythmical as before, and the momen-

On Various Uses of the Holding-Note 51

tary deviation will require a slight *crescendo* quite in the same way.

40 In each of the illustrations already given the holding-note has been either sustained or repeated. But its presence is equally evident when it is periodically returned to, as in Ex 39; this, however, being

Ex 39

merely one out of hundreds of interesting forms which composers have found for the application of this im-

52 *How to Accompany.*

portant device. In one form or other it is of such constant occurrence that the accompanist is rarely free from it for long together. His art will therefore largely consist of recognising it quickly in spite of any complicated aspect it may assume; and especially in drawing from it any feature which may serve to illustrate the text. Inherently the question is one of harmony; and the holding-notes described in this chapter are, after all, but elementary The student will find the question of notes common to various harmonies fully treated in the third portion of this work, to which he is referred for further improvement in it; and especially to the chapters which relate to modulation For the present, the subject may fairly be dismissed by the quotation of a harmonised figure simultaneously with the holding-note. This is exhibited in Ex. 40; where it will be

Ex. 40.

On Various Uses of the Holding-Note. 53

observed that the recurring note first takes the form of an organ-point yielding a particularly rich effect, afterwards passing in *diminuendo* to the upper part where the uniformity of treatment renders it prominent notwithstanding its softness

CHAPTER VI.

ON ACCOMPANIMENT WITH THE MELODY AS BASS OR INNER PART.

41. THE adoption of the melody as bass of the accompaniment is a somewhat cheap effect; much resorted to accordingly by inferior composers, and correspondingly welcome to inferior players. Fortunately, however, vulgar treatments of this device present no possible difficulty of execution; so that, by confining ourselves to artistic aspects of the matter, we shall be certain to include all that could require to be said in respect of them. The great attraction to the use of the melody as bass lies in the fact that it gives great support to the voice without obscuring it; and, providing this takes place in illustration of the text, and a special phrasing is naturally suggested, all is well. But, when the doubling of the voice is meaningless, the result is liable to be absurd; for, should the bass be in octaves, as most frequently happens, its weight requires that almost every note should have a distinct touch, in proportion to its height and

rhythmical prominence. The outcome is so ponderous that, in such cases, the harmony of the treble is power-

less to prevent the general effect from having a "unison" character; voice and octave-bass combined being an overbalance, assuming that all are treated equally. Only the falling of the bass with a slight *decrescendo*

Accompaniment with the Melody as Bass. 57

can allow the harmony to be felt at all; and, even without having that express intention in view, it adds so much grace to the phrase that classical composers, who are not at all partial to this effect as a rule, have some-

Ex. 42.

times used it very much to the purpose. A short instance is afforded by Ex. 41.

42. The melody may sometimes, though appearing as bass of the accompaniment, be repeated in dialogue with the voice instead of being used simultaneously

with it. By this means the heaviness is essentially removed; and the expression of the bass will, of course, be that of the vocal part. For a sample of this the reader may refer to Ex. 18; from which he will also see that, by employment of the melody as bass in this way, all "unison" effect also disappears.

43. Yet, even with such modification, the best song writers are chary of this means. The last example treats it, for instance, more as a purely instrumental effect of the "interspersed symphony" order; and it is also a purely instrumental effect when we find the melody appearing as bass during the opening symphony of a song, but not afterwards—an instance of which occurs in Ex. 42. Even here it will be noticed that it is used only in single notes; that being the usual plan adopted by good composers, in the absence of special need for some ponderous effect. In this way the lightness may be still further increased by the accompanist; when the melody, although forming his bass, is really in unison with the male voice, as, for instance, in Ex. 43. In such cases, by completely identifying the bass part with the voice, an illusion may be produced of increasing the latter's tone; which is precisely what the composer may be presumed to have had in view.

44. The next stage of this subject occurs in connection with the use of the melody as an inner-part; generally the tenor, but occasionally also the alto. The latter is more difficult for the accompanist, as a rule,

Accompaniment with the Melody as Bass. 59

Ex. 43.

on account of its requiring prominence for the middle notes of the harmony; and, bearing also its rarity in song accompaniment in mind, it does not seem likely that the player will ever excel without having recourse to solo work containing this special feature. For the purpose of obtaining this practice he may be specially referred to the later works of Brahms; or, for a single item, to the "Cradle-Song," Op 116, from which he will derive much benefit. In the meantime an instance of the introduction of the melody as alto of the accompaniment is given with Ex. 44.

Accompaniment with the Melody as Bass. 61

45 On the other hand, the use of the melody as tenor is quite a common occurrence; and forms not only a graceful style of accompaniment, but also a means of utilising the left hand to great advantage without much difficulty It leads to constant double notes in that quarter, however, and indifferent players often find this a great temptation to over-use of the thumb The degree to which the thumb may be required for the notes of the melody depends upon the size of hand, and it is therefore impossible to make any rule with regard to it; but it may nevertheless be well to mention that for thirds, fourths and fifths, the thumb cannot be a necessity in any case An instance of this style is presented by Ex 45.

46 The doubling of the melody is, of course, of tenor effect in this case; but the same disposition of the hands enables the doubling to be equally effected in the unison, when required. The last example, though in unison with tenor or bass, would be an oc-

Ex. 45.

tave lower than soprano or contralto; and this option is immaterial, as the effect is good in either case. But the character of the song would sometimes render such an alternative impossible. Ex. 46 is, for instance, the opening of a little nursery song, in which a charming simplicity is derived from doubling the child's voice in the unison; but in which a doubling in the octave below would have been entirely out of keeping The

Accompaniment with the Melody as Bass

Ex. 46.

use of the holding-note (treated in Chapter V) may here also be again observed.

47. In the same way the high pitch of the alto part in Ex 44 would sometimes be out of place; and, perhaps, a more usual and homely example of this device is that presented by Ex. 47; in which the alto part of the accompaniment is in unison with the male voice.

64 *How to Accompany.*

CHAPTER VII.

ON POLYPHONIC ACCOMPANIMENT.

48. THE counterpoint of polyphonic accompaniments is not usually either complicated or abstruse; and the instance of it presented in Ex. 10 (which was in three real parts) represents a fairly generous variety of motion in the several voices. It was mentioned, in connection with that example, that its vocal part was entirely independent, not being doubled by either of the three parts of the accompaniment; but that such was not always the case. Obviously a polyphonic accompaniment which is entirely independent of the vocal part demands great certainty from the singer, and corresponding care from the accompanist; especially with regard to the touch of such notes as might be calculated to lead to a faulty intonation if played too loud. It is no doubt the recognition of this fact by composers which leads to the part-writing in accompaniment being generally very simple—so simple indeed that there are frequent instances of its consisting of only *one* part besides the voice. Ex 48 is a pas-

Ex. 48.

sage of this kind (as the two hands, being in octaves, form only one real part) requiring not only to be played very lightly, but also to be most carefully adjusted to the voice. It is at all times desirable that the accompanist should read every note of the vocal part; no good accompaniment being possible under any other condition. But the rule to this effect is of exceptional rigour during polyphonic passages which do not double the voice; and any attempt to play these without a full grasp of the three-line score will surely lead to grief. They have generally little accentuation; appearing not so much to "accompany" the voice in the ordinary sense as to be an independent though sympathetic part. This style of performance is rendered natural by the prevalent "organ" character of such work; which favours a strictly legato treatment, and does not call for emphasis.

On Polyphonic Accompaniment. 67

49 The last was offered as an example in only two parts including the voice, but three is a more usual number and produces a very chaste and beautiful form of accompaniment. The ensemble is the same in conception as the organ "trio" for two manuals and pedal and no purer or more refined way of combining the voice and piano can possibly be imagined. An instance of its use is given with Ex 49

Ex 49.

50. This character of smoothness and softness may be taken as generally applicable to polyphonic accompaniments which are either independent of the voice, or in which the melody only occurs as an inner part; though of course a slightly increased demonstration is permissible in the latter case. But when the melody is doubled by forming the upper part of the instrumental polyphony the case is different. The legato character still prevails; but the accompaniment is no longer in hushed attendance upon the voice, since its own melody is identical with the latter. So long as the accompanist identifies his upper part with the voice-line with care and discretion he will be enabled from time to time to allow it a certain prominence; and, whenever he does so, the lower voices of his part should *crescendo* in sympathy, though always remaining a little behind in point of quantity of tone. Ex. 50 offers a fair sample of accompaniment of this kind, and presents also the conventional feature of an in-

On Polyphonic Accompaniment

determinate number of parts. Thus, at *(a)*, the tenor of the accompaniment suddenly ceases, and the number of parts is reduced for a time from four to three. But, at *(b)*, at a rise in the voice-part, they are increased to four again; thus showing that the polyphony of accompaniments is not necessarily so strict as in the previous examples and that the reduction and increase of the number of its parts is even counted upon for a *crescendo* and *decrescendo* in sympathy with the voice. The knowledge of this fact is obviously a most valuable guide to the player.

51. It is rare to find polyphony employed as accompaniment to an entire vocal piece; in fact, a feature of this description would nowadays be considered of quite antique character. The subject of the song will naturally determine the fact and extent of its employment; but, even without any special incentive, the desultory occurrence of polyphony is likely at any

moment, and is a thing therefore for which the player must continually be prepared.

52. The plain forms of accompaniment mentioned in the general survey of the first chapter have now been so far described that to go beyond the point at which we have arrived would encroach upon the domain either of choral music on the one hand or solo playing on the other. To take polyphony as an example, it is obviously an element which, in such circumstances, stands for a far higher development than can possibly happen in ordinary pianoforte accompaniment. As for the polyphony of solo work, the mere fact of its being self-sufficing creates an enormous difference; whilst that of choral music as a condensation of orchestral parts is entirely indeterminate and liable to be at times of extreme difficulty.

53. In the foregoing descriptions figuration has been purposely avoided, in order to allow of its being copiously and systematically dealt with in a special portion of this work. We have now therefore to deal, not with the differences between modes of accompaniment, but with the mechanics which apply equally to them all.

END OF PART I.

PART II
FIGURATED ACCOMPANIMENT

CHAPTER VIII.

ON THE MAJOR TRIAD AS BASIS FOR FIGURATION.

54. HAVING so far treated of varieties of material, we have now to consider how that material is lightened and shaded in practice, and how the mechanical difficulties created are to be approached. The question of harmony will not concern us very greatly for the moment as it is one reserved to be dealt with specially; but as figuration naturally requires some harmonic basis for its application it will be necessary to

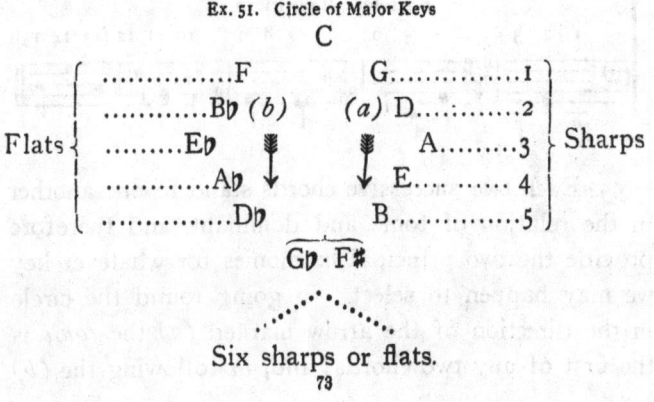

Ex. 51. Circle of Major Keys

Six sharps or flats.

stipulate at once for the reader's complete knowledge of the major triads. It will also be necessary for him to familiarise himself with the simple plan pursued, and upon which all future exercises will be based. We begin with the circle of major keys as in Ex. 51.

Ex. 52.

Progression of Major Triads in travelling round the circle of keys from left to right; or by successive dominants.

55. Each two successive chords stand to one another in the relation of tonic and dominant, and therefore provide the two principal harmonies for whatever key we may happen to select. In going round the circle in the direction of the arrow marked (*a*) the *tonic* is the first of any two chords; and, in following the (*b*)

Major Triad as Basis for Figuration.

arrow, the *dominant* comes first. Moreover, by selecting any chord as tonic and alternating it with the chords which lie on either side we introduce a third harmony; that, namely, of the subdominant.

56. We will begin by travelling round the circle in the direction of arrow *(a)*; or, that is to say, by suc-

Ex. 53. Chord Progressions.

Tonic	Dominant	Tonic.	Sub-Dominant	Tonic	Tonic	Dominant.	Tonic	Sub-Dominant	Tonic.
2	3	2	1	2	8	9	8	7	8
3	4	3	2	3	9	10	9	8	9
4	5	4	3	4	10	11	10	9	10
5	6	5	4	5	11	12	11	10	11
6	7	6	5	6	12	13	12	11	12
7	8	7	6	7	13	14	13	12	13

cessive dominants The bass will naturally be the same for each of the three positions of the triad; and twelve chords will, of course, suffice to bring us back to the starting point. Therefore, in Ex. 52, the chords are merely extended to fifteen for the purpose of showing how the same exercise may, if necessary, be carried through the next octave.

57. The reader should become practically familiar with this example; and, having done so, next proceed to form progressions in each key consisting of:

Tonic, dominant, subdominant.

In order to help him to do this, the table of numbers is offered (Ex. 53), illustrative of what has already been said of alternating the tonic harmony with that on either side of it.

58. The cadences formed from the above are exemplified in Ex. 54, as to the first four of them; the reader being left to carry out the remainder for himself. He will observe that the result is a series of half-cadences, while the application is to successive dominants, as in Ex. 52; but that it becomes a series

Major Triad as Basis for Figuration.

Ex. 55.

Progression of Major Triads in travelling round the circle of keys from right to left; or by successive subdominants.

How to Accompany.

of full cadences, if taken from the progression of sub-dominants shown in Ex. 55 Cadences resulting from the latter application are given with Ex. 56.

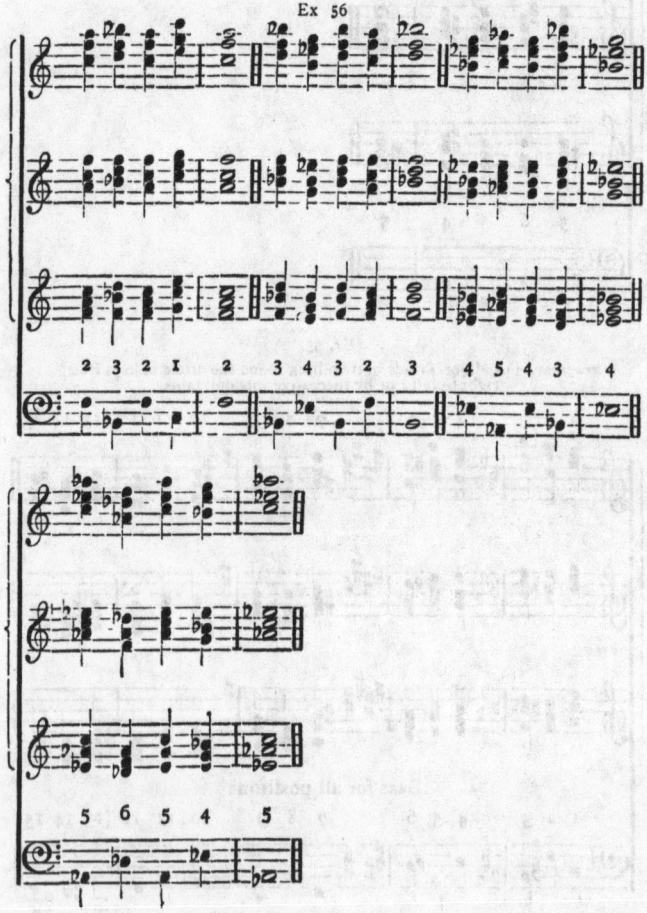

Major Triad as Basis for Figuration.

59. Now the object of all this is not to *teach* the triad harmony, the reader being already supposed to know that and a great deal more; but to supply a ready means of bringing each position of any triad under his complete mechanical control, as well as to familiarise him with the transition from any triad to that lying either on the dominant or subdominant side of it in the circle of keys. The exercises given are purposely restricted to essentials as to notes, besides which the progressions are taken in what appeared to be the most useful direction—though it must be remembered that others are available. As so much depends upon a complete mastery of this chapter, a few commencements are shown in Ex. 57 to 59, which the

Ex. 57.

80   *How to Accompany.*

zealous student will find it wise to utilise for further progress, after he has finished with the simple forms presented by Examples 52 and 55. Ex. 57 consists of exactly the same progressions as before, but with addition of the octave. In Ex 58 the positions are

varied; and this will not only afford additional practice if properly carried out, but also be an incentive to the student to invent other position-changes of the same harmony. Ex. 59 indicates a form of the same practice very advisable for larger hands, but which may also be undertaken by small ones with the aid of a greater or less dispersion according to necessity. In every case the same basses serve for three positions;

Major Triad as Basis for Figuration.

Ex 59.

and, if these exercises are properly carried through the keys until a high degree of mechanical fluency is attained, the whole of the subsequent instruction will be found to have become greatly facilitated.

CHAPTER IX.

ACCOMPANIMENTS FORMED FROM TRIPLET DISPERSIONS OF THE TRIAD.

60 THE means adopted for the figuration of chords are various; but the most serviceable on account of its lightness, and therefore the most usual, is the arpeggio. Taking the triads which we have just discussed as material, therefore, the simplest figuration would consist of dispersing the notes of which they are formed. Out of the many ways in which this may be done two will no doubt instantly occur to the reader; the plain dispersion upwards and downwards The elementary character of these two forms has naturally led to their very extensive use; and, of the two, the ascending dispersion may be said to enjoy the greater favour. It will be obvious that the triad without the octave lends itself most readily to triplet groups, whilst the addition of the octave converts the hand position into one more appropriate for groups of four semiquavers. Also, that hands and groups may both be used alternately; and in short that, with-

Accompaniments from Triplet Dispersions.

out having recourse to the slightest complication, it is open to us to apply several types of figuration to our triad material This is shown in Examples 60 and 61; which give eight elementary forms of triplet groups

Ex 60

for successive dominants and subdominants respectively; and, at the same time, exemplify how all figurations requiring practice are to be taken round the keys.

61. We now proceed to the practical application of the triplet group; and, firstly, for the production of a

How to Accompany.

Ex. 61

light guitar-like effect, in which it is mostly associated with staccato bass: see Ex. 62. This style of

Ex. 62.

accompaniment is generally in a cheerful degree of movement; but the character of expression mostly corresponds with the bass, which is sostenuto when the time is slower and the sentiment more meditative, as in Ex. 63. There we have a medium degree of seri-

ousness only; as, even with a sostenuto bass, this simple figuration does not lend itself to much solemnity. The accompanist, however, can generally at once trace the kind of expression to be given, according to the *degree* of the sostenuto, as well as by its association with chromatic modifications of the triad harmony. Two short cases of this kind are presented with Examples 64 and 65; and the attention of the reader is specially

drawn to the points marked *(a)* and *(b)* where chromatic alterations occur, because a good accompanist without giving those notes any merely vulgar accentua-

Accompaniments from Triplet Dispersions. 87

tion, will always know how to recognise the intention of their introduction.

62. It has been remarked that the ascending dispersion enjoys the greater favour, and the reason for this is that it forms an accompaniment pure and simple; whereas the descending dispersion, by commencing with the highest note, has a tendency to give prominence to the commencement of each beat and thus to appear to evolve a separate melody. This, of course, is very serviceable when any such separate melody is actually desired; and this is, moreover, a feature which very frequently happens. Sometimes a separate stem is given to the notes which go to form these progressions; but the accompanist must not depend upon such indication, and be always prepared to evolve from descending dispersions whatever meaning may attach to them, which can always be discovered by reference to the vocal part Two instances are

Ex. 66.

Ex. 67

given with Examples 66 and 67, the melodic progressions to be evolved from the accompaniment being indicated in small notes upon the vocal line, for extra clearness. In the second of these cases it will be observed that the progression arises from the middle note and is therefore a sort of inner melody. This is a very interesting question and one to which the student

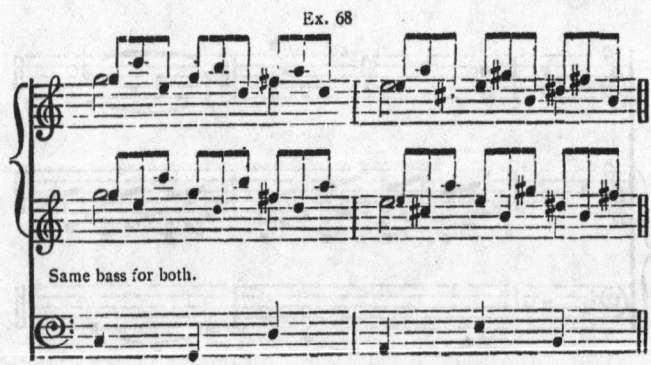

Ex. 68

Same bass for both.

Accompaniments from Triplet Dispersions. 89

should give earnest attention, as figurations of this kind abound in the works of all good composers. In order to assist him in this direction, two such progressions are shown with Examples 68 and 69. In these examples it will be observed that the inner melody consists simply of descending tones; this being merely for exercise, as there is obviously no limit to the number of possible designs Independently of separate

Ex. 69.

melody the same form of accompaniment is sometimes made use of for gentle reiteration of the holding note, as in Ex. 70; or, for support of the voice, by doubling,

Ex. 70.

as in Ex. 71. Such simple devices generally mean that something important is going on in the bass at the same time. It is not only a most improving form of

Accompaniments from Triplet Dispersions. 91

practice, but also a highly entertaining one to carry such designs through the keys; and the student who has the courage to form this habit will be astonished at the facility resulting from it. Examples 72 and 73

exhibit how the two last passages should be applied to the circle of keys, and this forms a suitable conclusion to triplet dispersions of the triad; for, although various other dispersions may be formed, they are not only of more exceptional and less useful character, but are entirely amenable to the same explanations.

92   *How to Accompany.*

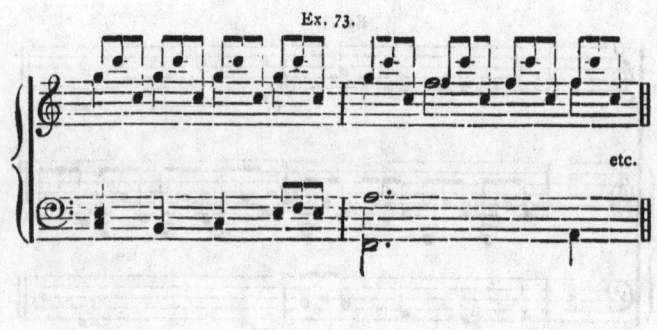

CHAPTER X.

ACCOMPANIMENTS FORMED FROM FURTHER TRIAD DISPERSIONS.

63 THE further arpeggio distribution of the triad naturally introduces us to the four semiquaver group; and, in ordinary course, we should begin with the plain ascending and descending series, as we did in the case of triplets. But there is a distinction to be drawn, for the reason that the ascending series of four has a certain coarseness which deprives it of the favour of the best composers, whilst the descending series induces such emphasis upon its upper note as to restrict its use to somewhat exceptional occasions. Of the former it can scarcely be necessary to give an example as it is not only an ungraceful form of accompaniment but can never present the slightest difficulty to the player; but of the latter, two typical instances may be found in Examples 74 and 75. Each of these is demonstrative in its own way, the first in emphasising the beats and the second in sustaining the effect of the holding note; the difficulty to the player being to secure a touch suffi-

How to Accompany.

Ex 74.

Ex 75.

Accompaniments from Triad Dispersions. 95

ciently light to enable the contrasts to be felt, with a small amount of accent in either case. These are special effects; and, for ordinary accompaniment, the really graceful forms of semiquaver groups may be said to begin when one or more notes are employed for the return, as in Ex. 76. Here, only one such note is used, the result being that the accentuation is extremely gentle; and inexperienced accompanists fre-

Ex 76.

quently give too much accent, simply on account of the lowest notes mostly falling to the thumb. If, however, accompanists will regard the number of notes used in returning as the measure of the accentuation they will be saved from this error; and in Ex. 77, with six-note

Ex. 77.

groups in an octave position, we have an instance of accompaniment in which a slight increase of accent at the commencement of the beat is justifiable. The breadth of the wave, or, in other words, the interval covered by the entire position also contributes to this feature; so that, had this interval been wider, the amount of accentuation might have been even more. From this it follows that a rippling effect is produced by a number of small ascents and returns; and that, in such cases, there will be scarcely any appreciable accent at all, as in Ex. 78. Thus, although the whole of the semiquaver groups hitherto have been of the

Accompaniments from Triad Dispersions. 97

Ex. 78.

nature of pure accompaniment, the examples from 74 to 78 present varying amounts of accentuation for the beat; and, in each case, the player can trace the requisite mode of performance in the form of the accompaniment itself.

64. We have now to consider the application to the groups of four and six of the same procedure as that shown in Examples 66 and 67 as applied to the triplet. It was then explained that the result of giving

the accent to an intermediate note was to establish an inner voice in the accompaniment; though it does not always follow that this part requires to be brought prominently forward, as the groups may still be a mere figuration. The question is: "How is the player to know whether any special phrasing is required or not?" To answer this he has only to see whether any evident feature of interest is set up by this series in connection with the vocal part. Thus in Ex. 79 it would be diffi-

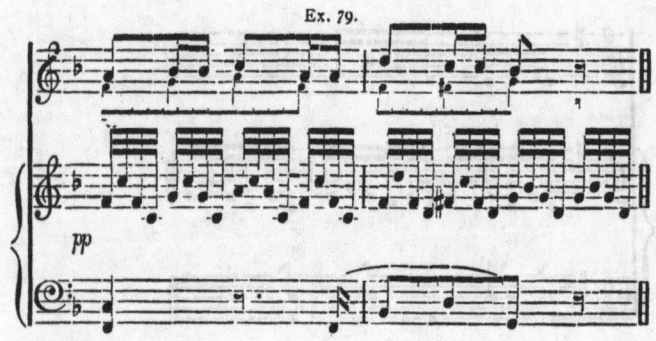

Ex. 79.

cult not to see that the first notes of the groups form really a sort of alto part as indicated by the small notes on the voice line, and that a faint prominence is to be accorded them on that account—a prominence not produced by positive accentuation, but by subordinating the remainder of the group.

65. Such inner progressions stand midway between plain accompaniment and the ostinato motive. Of the latter there are many kinds; but they may be broadly

Accompaniments from Triad Dispersions. 99

divided into those which rely upon the mere notes of the harmony and those which call chromatic changes and other expedients to their aid. The last lie beyond the stage of the subject of which we are now treating, but there is no lack of artistic design capable of being wrought from the simple notes of the harmony. As ostinato motives give a certain aspect to the notation their existence is bound to be observed at once; and the player should endeavour to secure a uniform fingering for all of them. The selection of this will of course depend upon size of hand and general technical power; but, whatever it may be, uniformity is desirable; because uniformity of fingering is the best way to make sure of uniformity of touch, and, without the latter, the beauty of an ostinato motive is very seriously injured. Thus, in Ex. 80, there are some hands quite capable of executing the motives with a single position; and, providing they can all be performed in that way, that is well. But a hand which is obliged to

Ex 80.

use two positions should *always* do so, even when the extent of the passage might enable him mechanically to play it with only one; for the sake of giving the fingers the same rhythmical positions.

66. Another feature of the ostinato motive is that, while in continual sympathy with the voice part, it still has its own expression. Thus, in Ex. 80, the semiquaver group is commenced with extreme lightness, the expression of each bar being:

the intensity of which will slightly vary with the width of the intervals employed, but never attain sufficient force to intrude upon the voice.

67. The reader must not conclude from this precision that ostinato motives are difficult. What renders them easy is that their artistic performance is always subject to the same principles, so that when

Accompaniments from Triad Dispersions. 101

once the player has formed the necessary habit he applies it equally to all.

68. It may now be considered that the student should no longer require special examples to enable him to work matters round the circle of keys. In this connection he may be advised that all the hints given upon the subject, both in Chapter IX and previously, are here again perfectly applicable.

CHAPTER XI.

ACCOMPANIMENTS FORMED FROM BROKEN CHORDS.

69. IF we closely examine what are called "broken chords" we shall find them to consist of a combination of chord and arpeggio The most usual forms in which the accompanist is likely to meet with them are those of either successive double-notes or of double and single-notes alternately. A happy instance of the first is shown in Ex. 81; where every two note combination is a chord, and, at the same time, part of an

Ex 81.

Accompaniments from Broken Chords.

arpeggio It is of course natural to finger such groups in the same way as the chords of which they are the distribution, but this creates a danger with some players of not duly securing every repetition when the upper note in one case becomes the lower in the next, and vice versa.

70. Accompaniments consisting of alternate double and single notes are more usual; and, as the alternation is rarely if ever strictly followed, the player may

regard occasional returns to single notes as indicating that less tone is required. This is another case in which accompanying differs from solo playing; for, in the latter, this feature would not have the same meaning—the fact being that really skilful accompaniment is an art of great refinement calling for so many varieties of touch that it would be impossible to burden the notation with their full indication. Take, for instance, the simple passage shown in Ex. 82. In this

Ex 82.

case a *decrescendo* is indicated as the single notes are about to enter; but, had it not been so, the intention would have been equally evident, and the accompanist must be so habituated to these graduations of touch as not to be obliged to give them special thought in each individual case.

71. As the composer is thus presumed to desire less tone when he reduces the number of notes, it follows by the same reasoning that when he increases the num-

Accompaniments from Broken Chords.

ber he requires more—that is to say *slightly* more than the mere additional notes would imply, by way of assisting the poetic intention. A keen eye for such features is of the greatest value, as the effects are very often such as we should not otherwise have expected. In Ex. 83, for instance, with a falling voice at the

Ex 83.

third bar we have an extra note given to the harmonies of the accompaniment. The increase of tone required is not sufficient to justify the use of the conventional

106   *How to Accompany.*

signs, but the additional chord-note indicates it exactly.

72. Such delicate means of indicating tone graduation apply naturally to soft passages principally, but it is obvious that they are also capable of assisting materially in other cases; and where a broad and demonstrative *crescendo* is required it is rendered more effective by a simultaneous increase in the number of notes. No instruction is here required, however, as

Accompaniments from Broken Chords. 107

such features are too patent to allow of their being missed. An instance is presented by Ex. 84.

73. The alternate single and double note is a very fertile means for the creation of set figures of accompaniment when chromatics are admitted; but, whilst these figures remain within the harmony, they never present much difficulty. One of the most familiar forms is that shown in Ex. 85, where the double notes

Ex. 85.

follow the melody immediately after the beat. Sometimes an upper part on the bass line will assist the melody as well, as was the case with this kind of accompaniment in Ex. 45; but in both it will be noticed that the double note precedes the single one and that it follows the note of the melody. It is well that the player should mark thoroughly the difference of effect caused by the double notes of the accompaniment occurring simultaneously with the melody, because this will be a caution to him to play them very lightly in order to avoid any approximation to an effect which he does not want. Thus Ex. 86 is a fragment from

Ex. 86.

a nursery song where of course the childishness of giving out the melody with double notes is quite appropriate; but equally unsuitable elsewhere, for the same reason.

74. As to the opposite case—that in which the single precedes the double note—nothing could be more remarkable than the difference of effect caused by this reversal. The form thus created is not only one which lends itself most readily to a staccato touch, but also to the development of counter melody; and the numberless interesting applications of it render it difficult to do justice to the matter with a short example. Ex 87, however, will probably show the reader what is intended to be implied; as the separate melody of the accompaniment, the staccatissimo touch, and the freedom of the voice are in it alike evident.

Accompaniments from Broken Chords. 109

Ex. 87.

Good - bye! . . . . .

75. The alternate double and single-note is also much adopted as a convenient form of tremolo, and instances of its use have already occurred in connection with Examples 17, 18 and 41. In each of these, however, the number of notes is unregulated; the desired effect being that of a gentle sostenuto. A tremolo of this description either proceeds "misterioso" or is broken by an occasional *sforzando* for dramatic effect; otherwise, merely sympathising with the general outline of expression. The case is different with the regulated tremolo; which has to be rhythmised, as in Ex. 88. Such forms are mostly associated with quick movement—at all events in good compositions, as the conversion of them into slow figures has a most puerile effect.

76 Another kind of tremolo occasionally used in accompaniment may also be mentioned as consisting of a filling up of the weak beats of the bar only, thus

Ex. 88.

producing an effective agitato—providing it is executed with sufficient lightness and rapidity. It necessitates that the strong beats of the bar should be well represented, and this happens most favourably with a separate bass melody, as in Ex. 89.

77. The student must remember that the foregoing are merely a few of the most usual designs formed with broken chords, selected not with any view of

Accompaniments from Broken Chords.

exhausting the subject (which would be impossible) but for the purpose of providing him with a basis of study for any forms which he may encounter in actual practice.

CHAPTER XII.

RHYTHMICAL FIGURES OF ACCOMPANIMENT.

78. WE have seen how lightness of accompaniment is attained by dispersion of the harmony, and how this lightness is graduated by the introduction of double notes. The latter, as compared with single notes, incline to a rhythmical meaning; which, while the accent falls to them, is not observed, but which, in a passage like that of Ex. 87, compels great care to avoid an effect of syncopation.

79. But we must distinguish between mere lightness of *touch* and lightness of the *rhythm* itself. Thus, in Ex. 113, the touch is light while the rhythm is ponderous; whilst, in Exs. 90 to 92, the rhythm is light, whilst the amount of emphasis required in phrasing is rather more than usual. These are "rhythmic figures" of accompaniment, produced from repeated chords; and of such we have now to treat.

80. The simplest figure formed with repeated chords is that of the "measured tread" shown in Ex. 38, in which absolute equality of touch is the desideratum.

Rhythmical Figures of Accompaniment. 113

But, when the step consists of alternate notes of different length, the emphasis of the longer note is slightly increased; and this emphasis, coupled with the inequality of time, gives a skipping effect in fairly quick time; as in Ex. 90 Just as weariness was ex-

pressed by equality of touch and time in Ex. 38, cheerfulness is here the result of inequality; but, in order to play this well, it is the lightness and blitheness of the quavers which we have most to think of, as the strong beats are sure to take care of themselves. This form of accompaniment in a quick movement does not require the crotchet to be held; but the contrary happens in a slow movement, where it is usually played *tenuto*. In each case it is the prevailing feature of expression; and, as such, requires care—either as to the blithesome quaver of the quick time, or as to the full sostenuto crotchet of the sorrowful andante. An instance of the latter is given with Ex. 91.

114 *How to Accompany.*

81. The next figure of accompaniment produced rhythmically by the aid of repeated notes is that in which a semiquaver is taken from the crotchet and, by forming a double percussion with the quaver, produces a galloping effect. Thus, the three figures so far exemplified may be shown as under:

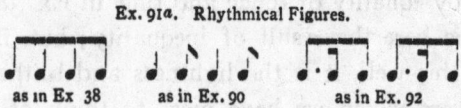

Such figures as these are mostly characteristic of the songs in which they occur, and are therefore liable to continue for some time. The last requires a special looseness of wrist; and the player will find himself able to avoid fatigue by advancing his fingers upon the keys for the second of the two rapid notes.

82. It will be remembered that some arpeggios form a *mere* accompaniment whilst others contain features of their own; and it is the same with repeated chords,

Ex. 92.

some forms of which provide merely a harmonic texture or background to give the melody greater effect. This is the common expedient of inferior composers; but with good writers it is rare to find complete absence of redeeming feature. Thus, in Exs. 30 and 43, there was a special interest in the bass; and the nearest approach to mere blank chord repetition to be met with in a good composer is shown in Exs. 93 and

Ex. 93.

94; though, even in them, a slight design is to be traced. Thus, in Ex 94 the repetitions are taken by

the hands alternately; which comes very close to forming a rhythmical figure, as may be perceived from Ex. 95, which is merely a slight extension of the same

idea. Fortunately, these simple repetitions can require no instruction (except that of avoiding them as much as possible); but it may be useful to show

Rhythmical Figures of Accompaniment.

Ex. 96

How to Accompany.

that, even when used for mere accompaniment, they can be rendered full of interest, as in Ex. 96, in which the several features are indicated for the student's guidance.

83. Other forms of chord repetition consist of light pulsations following a strong beat in the bass; which however are so easy to play that we may consider ourselves dispensed from doing more than give samples

Ex. 97.

Rhythmical Figures of Accompaniment. 119

Ex. 98.

of them. These will be found in Examples 97 and 98.

84. Sometimes chord repetitions are effectively used in syncopations; either palpitating across the beats of the voice or alternating with a moving bass. This is a form which specially lends itself to gradual changes of harmony; as will be seen when the separate subject comes to be treated later. In the mean-

Ex. 99.

time, Ex. 99 will serve as a sample of this kind of accompaniment.

85. Mention must finally be made of chord repetitions in cross-rhythms; the most familiar use of which consists of three against two—as under:

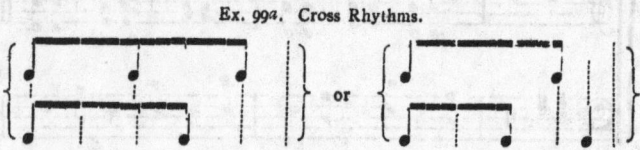

Ex. 99a. Cross Rhythms.

The accompanist must in such cases take his time from the *greater* number; or, in other words, he must adjust the two to the three, and not vice versa. No more detailed adjustment with the voice is desirable than that with the latter's *full* beat—in fact it would be peculiarly distressing to a good singer to be sensible of any mechanical adjustment at all. Ex. 100 will provide an instance of ordinary kind only, but

Ex. 100.

Rhythmical Figures of Accompaniment. 121

sufficient for the purpose; for, although cross-rhythms include an infinity of possibilities, they are not much in favour for purposes of accompaniment, and "three against two" will be all that the accompanist is likely to require, except in extraordinary cases.

CHAPTER XIII.

ALTERNATED HAND-MOTION IN ACCOMPANIMENT.

86. ALTERNATION of hand-motion may be regarded as one form of dispersion, and hence (like the dispersion of chords by arpeggio) is resorted to in order to obtain lightness without diminishing the fullness of the harmony. Alternation in one sense has already appeared in several of the cases given, but only in Exs. 14*b*, 15, 32 and 99 does it occur within the meaning here intended; because in those instances the alternation takes place at equal distances of time. In Exs. 45, 85 and 98 we have alternations of 1 against 2; in Nos. 5 and 93 we have 1 against 3; whilst in Nos. 81 and 83 we have 1 against 5. The several instances will serve to show the importance of alternation in accompaniment, however, as well as to point to the many graduations to which it is subject; but they all belong to a class of accompaniment in which one part (generally the bass) serves as rhythmical support for subdivisions of the beat. On the other hand we might fairly regard Exs. 94 and 95 as strict alter-

Alternated Hand-Motion in Accompaniment. 123

nations, being repetitions of 2+2 and 4+4; though these are better classed as rhythmical figures.

87 The increase in the rate of motion produced by alternation often contributes more to the lightness of an accompaniment than the distribution of the harmony in the form of arpeggio. Let the reader compare, for instance, the accompaniments of examples 101 and 102; and he will find that in the former,

Ex. 101.

Ex. 102.

although the chords are small, the sluggish motion contributes a heaviness from which the latter is exempt.

88 Sometimes alternation is resorted to in order to support the voice in the unison without incurring the blankness of merely doubling the voice part, and with a view to rendering the later harmony more effective, as in Ex 14*b* On the other hand the contrary may occur; and the alternation be employed to make the unison prominent and throw the harmony into the background, as in Ex. 15. The student will thus perceive that alternate hand motion in itself is neutral, and equally ready to lend itself to all effects. Sometimes, for example, the unison effect to which it is called in aid does not concern the voice at all, as in Ex. 103, in which case the accompaniment requires most careful handling. But unison effects, after all, are of secondary importance compared with adorn-

Ex 103.

Alternated Hand-Motion in Accompaniment. 125

ments of the voice part, as in Ex. 104; and to the variety of which there is literally no end.

Ex. 104.

89. Alternation is also very frequently employed for increased brilliancy; but, as the alternation often consists of merely separating component parts of what, if played together, would form quite simple harmony, cases of this kind may here be excluded as requiring no special instruction. In good composers such plain

alternation is somewhat rare; occasion being generally taken by them to associate some other feature of interest with the alternation Ex. 105 will serve as a

sample of simple alternation such as we are liable to meet with in works which are well written; and in it the student will observe that an independent melodic progression occurs, greatly aiding the general effect.

Alternated Hand-Motion in Accompaniment. 127

There is in fact nothing more distressing than puerile reiteration without any associated feature; and, even in the simple cadence offered in Ex. 106, an independent feature of accompaniment is presented.

Ex. 106.

90. It has already been said that alternations of other equal numbers partake of the nature of rhythmical figures. But, for the sake of regularity, it may be well to supplement those already given by others to complete the series Examples 94 and 95 presented instances of the alternations of two and four respectively; and a sample of three in alternation will be found in Ex. 107. A slight throw of the wrist compasses the whole of the three notes in this case, which should, as a group, produce the effect of a *quaver*, with tremulous expression. The last note is therefore inexpressibly light; its lightness being just as much a feature as its weight would have been in the event of its falling upon the accent. Ex. 108 is a sample of

Ex. 107.

Ex. 108.

the latter kind in alternations of two and two; and in it the beats marked *, although of secondary normal strength, receive the greater accent.

91. It remains now to speak of those alternations which, while consisting of equal numbers, are not performed in equal time. This has a natural connection with the preceding because the greater time is generally accorded to the weaker beat for the purpose of

giving it prominence. Of course this may happen in many degrees, but the most important relation for practical purposes is that of one to two, an instance of which is presented by Ex. 109.

Ex. 109.

92. This completes the alternation question, with the exception of alternation which arises through dividing between the two hands passages which are in reality one. It must be obvious, however, that, as such alternation depends upon mechanics, and in fact need not be adopted by good players at all, it does not form any part of the artistic subject.

CHAPTER XIV.

OSTINATO FIGURES OF ACCOMPANIMENT.
(RHYTHMICAL.)

93. BEFORE embarking upon the question of ostinato figures of accompaniment, either rhythmical or characteristic, it is desirable to make a slight survey of what has been already done, in order that the reader may quite understand the relation of these chapters to the subject in general.

(a) First, we had absolutely simple and subordinate accompaniment; represented by unison, phrase-chord and plain harmonisation.

(b) Next, we had the introduction of the holding note, transference of the melody to bass or inner parts, and polyphonic harmonisation.

(c) Then we had the dispersion of the harmony, either by simple distribution as arpeggio, by broken chords or by hand-alternation; with or without the appearance of separate melodic progressions.

(d) And we have also had rhythmic harmonisation, as evolved from repeated chords.

94. The utility of this review is to point out that, although the above present some interesting features of accompaniment, they all exist for the purpose of adding grace and intensity of expression to the vocal part, and not as integral portions of the compositions to which they refer. From one point of view they may be regarded as essential; but that is only on account of the importance of their addition to the *ensemble*, and does not prevent their contribution to the effect being, after all, of the nature of an *addition* to it But, when we approach the ostinato figure of accompaniment, we have to deal with what is really a *duet* with the voice; and, although we shall, of course, begin with ostinato figures of the simplest kind, the vocal line under those conditions can no longer be regarded as self-sufficing.

95 It is the business of the accompanist to read, as it were *behind* the rhythmical figure, the simple element from which it is formed; in order to give it the same expression. Thus in the following example:

Ex. 110. Formation of simple rhythmical figures.

132   *How to Accompany.*

(c) has the same expression as *(a)*, and *(d)* the same expression as *(b)* under ordinary circumstances. This means of course that the notes are not simply read mechanically, but that, for example, the lightness of the quaver of *(b)** is represented by a blithe manner of performing the two semiquavers at *(d);* and so on. The figures shown in Ex. 110 are practically exhibited in Ex. 111.

Ex. 111.

---

* This feature occurred also in connection with Ex. 90 q.v.

Ostinato Figures of Accompaniment. 133

Ex 112.

96. This principle of bearing the *origin* of the figure in mind is most important for the accompanist, as it influences his performance considerably. Thus, the rhythmical form of the figure shown in Ex. 112 is simply:

and it will be patent to every reader that the player who accepts this is the ideal expression will evolve an effect quite different from that of the mechanical note reader.

97. But an even more powerful reason for discerning the rhythmic origin behind the figure lies in the fact that it is much easier to do so; for, by this means, apparently complex figures are precisely those which are generally seen to spring from the simplest elements. Take, for example, the figure shown in Ex. 113, which is all upon a single chord to the figure:

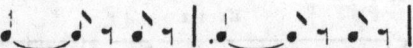

98. The difficulty of playing ostinato figures lies in fulfilling the duty of making them thoroughly appre-

Ex 113

ciated by the listener, and, at the same time, not allowing them to become intrusive; but here again a close

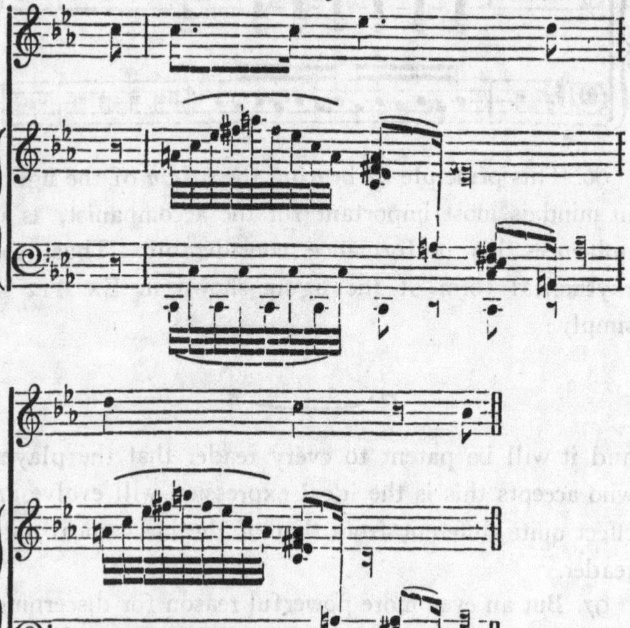

Ostinato Figures of Accompaniment. 135

adherence to the rhythmic origin is extremely helpful, as it forms the best safeguard and support for the singer. This especially applies to figures which are at all heavy or complicated. As for the lighter forms, when they traverse the voice part or venture upon notes foreign to the harmony, although the slightness of accompaniment may render it not quite so compulsory to bear the rhythm of origin in mind, it will still be far better to do so; as, for instance, in Ex. 114 where

the player who is conscious that the notes bracketed are the distribution of a governing element in the rhythm will be sure to give a better accompaniment than one who does not do so.

99. All these rhythmic figures are within the harmony; and, with the introduction of passing notes and kindred means of variety, we approach the characteristic figure which is the subject of the next chapter.

Exception may, however, be made of the melodic inflection marked * in Ex. 115; which is clearly a rhyth-

mical figure, being an elaboration of the dotted crotchet. And here, finally, the same principle applies, for, by bearing the dotted crotchet as the rhythm of origin in mind, the accompanist cannot fail to render the figure with a slight *diminuendo* on each occasion and by doing so interpret the composer's evident intention.

CHAPTER XV.

OSTINATO FIGURES OF ACCOMPANIMENT.
(CHARACTERISTIC.)

100. WE have already had a sample of the characteristic figure, in the rippling accompaniment of Ex. 78; but, in that case, restriction to the mere notes of the harmony caused the leading traits of this kind of figure to appear absent. This was also the restrictive feature in Ex. 81; which, as a harp accompaniment, was also fully characteristic. These are exceptions; for, as a rule, the characteristic figure draws upon *independent* melodic progressions, though only as a result of the nature of the idea to be expressed. Thus, if we apply this principle to the case before us we shall see at once that, whilst the ripple of the running brook is well represented *within* the harmony, the flowing waves of open waters call for a figure more indicative of motion; and that the expression sought by means of passing notes is, after all, a question of degree only, as the parent idea—that of running or flowing water—is, in both cases precisely the same. This being well

understood, let the reader compare the "ripple" of Ex. 48 with the "flow" of Ex. 116.

101. The songs in which these figures appear are accompanied by them throughout, without the slightest break; as any such interruption would have been obviously inconsistent with the idea to be expressed. The ostinato figure does not assume such rigid continuity in all cases, but it always constitutes a main

trait of the piece in which it occurs; and the pertinacious use of the one passage sometimes causes the composer to permit certain collisions with the voice part which he would probably not tolerate were the notes in question appearing only in a single instance. It is therefore highly necessary to read the voice part simultaneously with the accompaniment, as a sympathetic performance demands the delicate handling of such progressions. Thus, even in Ex. 116, which is by no means a special instance, the notes marked * might have a coarse effect by being unduly enforced, even though the passage, considered as solo work, might be well played. It is, in fact, quite possible to be a good solo player, and, at the same time, a bad accompanist.

102. It is very desirable to use uniform fingering for ostinato figures, even in spite of any slight mechanical difficulty. Without this, it is both impossible to rhythmise always in precisely the same way and to graduate the touch in sympathy with the rise and fall of the voice part with sufficient delicacy. Ex. 117 is representative of the "whirl" of the spinning-wheel, and in it the reader may notice the slight modifications of the intervals in order to accommodate the harmony, though without disturbing the outline of the figure.

103. Ostinato figures are, however, not all of this continuous description, nor have they necessarily the fixed purpose of representing anything *audible* at all.

140 How to Accompany.

Ex 117

Ostinato Figures of Accompaniment. 141

They may, on the contrary, be merely introduced as a part of the composer's design; and without possessing any further reference to the words than a general appropriateness. In such cases they are neither so long retained nor so exactly reproduced; and it follows of course that the accompanist has also a greater freedom in their treatment. Ex. 118 affords a fair instance of this description; especially as it is one of *two* figures which occur in the same song; contrasting with, and relieving one another mutually. This is a

142 *How to Accompany.*

Ex. 118

First figure

type of vocal piece with which it is important that the accompanist should become familiar; but the only intelligent manner of doing so is to mark the contrasting features of the two figures, with a view to their realisation in performance. For his instruction therefore the second figure of the same song is presented by Ex. 119, and his attention is called to the following points of contrast:

(*a*) The first figure is in longer notes.

Ostinato Figures of Accompaniment. 143

Ex 119

(b) It is entirely confined to the notes of the chord in each case.

(c) The doubling in the octave shows that special lightness is not desired.

(d) The bass has considerable motion.

104. An opposite list will not be necessary, as it will surely be sufficient to say that in every one of the above respects the second figure presents a contrary feature. The beauty of this when well rendered may be easily conceived; but the first means of arriving at it is to *understand* exactly how it is produced.

105. Sometimes the number of set figures is greater than two; when, of course, the same method is to be applied to all of them. Vocal pieces frequently contain more of such features in proportion to the degree of excitement and intensity of expression to which they attain; and the accompanist may fairly expect the climax to occur during the figure which is *most florid*—though this is not always the case. But, wherever the climax occurs, he should know it before he begins to play; in order, from it, to regulate the touch for the whole of the remainder.

106. In conclusion of this chapter attention may once more be drawn to the importance of uniform fingering for ostinato figures by a very simple illustration. If, for instance, the player begins Ex. 118 with:

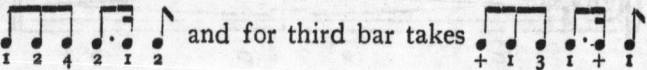

he endangers the perfect rendering of the phrase, without even gaining a mechanical advantage. The solo player is more or less justified in securing his mechanics *first*, but not so the accompanist; and the bearing of this principle in mind makes all the difference in the rendering of a song accompaniment.

END OF PART II.

END OF PART I.

PART III
PRACTICAL HARMONY FOR ACCOMPANISTS

CHAPTER XVI.

ON THE MINOR TRIAD IN ACCOMPANIMENT.

107. IN opening the second section of this work we were obliged to devote a first chapter to explanation of the workings of the *major* triad; as, without some basis, the subject of figuration could not be proceeded with. That chapter forms also an opening to the present section; and, now that we are dealing with accompanist's harmony as a separate subject, and having already, as stated, dealt with the major triad, it is obvious that the *minor* triad comes next in order. We proceed, therefore, at once with the circle of minor keys, upon the same plan as that pursued, in Ex. 51, for the major.

108. Each two successive chords are in the relation of tonic and dominant, precisely as explained in Chapter VIII; but the dominant is always major, even in a minor key, so that attention must be given to that fact in the formation of cadences. Ex. 120 presents the circle of successive dominants in minor keys after the same method as Ex. 52 in major keys; but, in the

150   How to Accompany

Ex 119a   Circle of Minor Keys.

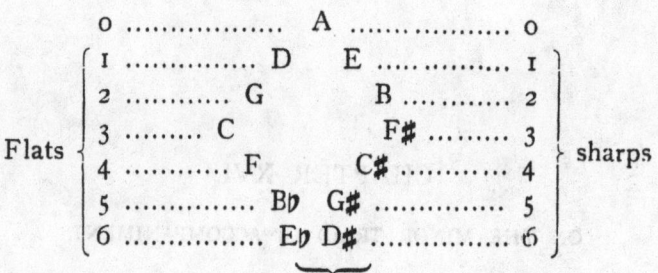

Ex 120.
Progression of Minor Triads in travelling round the circle of keys
from left to right; or by successive dominants.

Bass for all positions.

On the Minor Triad in Accompaniment.

cadences of Ex. 121, the sign * is attached to triads exercising the vocation of dominant for the time being, and which are accordingly major.

How to Accompany.

Ex 122

Progression of Minor Triads in travelling round the circle of keys from right to left; or by successive sub dominants.

On the Minor Triad in Accompaniment. 153

109. All the instruction of Chapter VII as to cadences also applies, so that we may immediately

Ex. 123.

pass on to refer to Ex. 122, which exhibits the circle of successive subdominants in minor keys, after the manner of Ex. 55 for major keys; as also to the cadences shown in Ex. 123, in which the dominants, being major, are marked * as before.

110. By the light of the instruction contained in Part II we need now be no longer restricted to the application of these triads to figurations entirely *within* the harmony; but shall proceed at once to carry them through the keys on the basis of the characteristic figure shown in Ex. 116. This will be done by successive *sub*dominants, at first, in order not to complicate the matter with major thirds. But, on the other hand, the passage in question is taken all round the keys in each of the *three* positions; as will be found exhibited in Exs. 124, 125 and 126 respectively.

Ex. 124

On the Minor Triad in Accompaniment. 155

156 *How to Accompany.*

Ex. 125.

On the Minor Triad in Accompaniment 157

Ex 126.

On the Minor Triad in Accompaniment. 159

111. The improving character of this form of practice can require no demonstration, and it is merely for the sake of making matters clear that one example is carried out in full, as the whole operation is one which should be worked mentally by the student; and in doing this he will not only be increasing his facility in manipulating triads but also preparing the way for his future success in transposition.

112. The experience of even one such exercise is so improving that for a second (for which purpose we select the characteristic figure of Ex. 117) it will be sufficient to score the three positions above the bass as in Ex. 127.

Ex 127.

160 *How to Accompany.*

On the Minor Triad in Accompaniment. 161

Ex. 128

113. The student may now vary the exercise by making each alternate chord major, and thus giving it a dominant relation to the key which follows. This is shown in Ex. 128, which is really a modification of Ex. 125. It will be observed that two forms *(a)* and *(b)* are given; but the second may be considered as an alternative reserved for more advanced students. For the latter it may specially be mentioned that providing the outline of the figure is preserved all that need be done is to see that skips take place within the chord. Readers are advised to use this form if possible, however, on account of the practice it affords in the augmented second of the harmonic minor scale.

114. When treating of major triads we took occasion to pass on to the more extended positions exhibited in Exs. 57 to 59. It is obvious that these also apply to minor triads, and are equally improving as practice in minor keys; but, as no new facts are involved, a further example is unnecessary. The same may be said of the simple arpeggio figurations shown in Exs. 60 and 61, which should also be carried out in the minor; as also of the figurations containing an inner melodic progression as exhibited in Exs. 68 and 69. All these are here omitted for the sake of brevity, and as having been already explained; but they must be quite understood to be entirely as essential to the working of the minor triad as of the major; and the earnest student is even recommended to give a preference of practice to the minor mode, in order to cor-

rect the common fault of not being sufficiently familiar with it. In carrying out this idea he need not confine himself to the examples here given, which are necessarily spare on account of limited space; but should single out for special practice the figurations of any songs in the minor mode which he may happen to accompany, by carrying them round the circle of keys, after the manner shown in Exs. 124 to 126. Exercise of this description is irksome only at first; besides which it is well to remember that the irksomeness only arises on account of the very deficiencies which this form of study is specially designed to correct.

CHAPTER XVII.

TRIAD POSITIONS REQUIRED IN ACCOMPANIMENT.

115. As the triad consists of two thirds above a bass it follows that either of these thirds may represent the full chord for the time being. Thus, should the accompanist meet with the major third, his sense of the context must guide him as to whether this stands for the lower portion of a major, or for the upper portion of a minor triad. Or, should he meet with a minor third only, this is equally liable to represent the upper portion of a major, or the lower portion of a minor, triad. This is shown in the following example:

Ex 129.

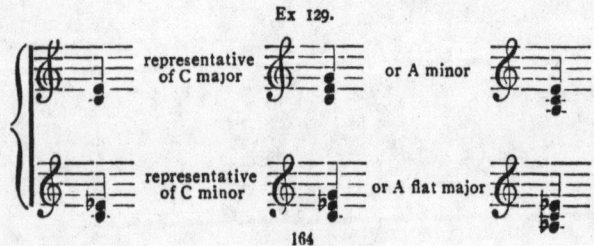

Triad Positions Required in Accompaniment. 165

116. The accompanist will find it particularly useful to scrutinise the intervals of which the various chords are built, as familiarity with their outward aspects will not only aid him in ordinary reading but also in transposing. The vagueness of the third in indication of the chord-root is shown above; but, when the octave is added and the interval of a fourth thereby presented (as shown in the following example), the player is able to accept its upper note as the natural bass of the chord.

Ex. 130.

117. Even these few preliminary words will suffice to show that the same harmony is liable to present itself to the accompanist under a variety of aspects. So much is known to every player, but without the extent being realised to which this variety proceeds. Thus, without going to extremes, and merely counting such ordinary dispositions of the notes as are liable to be encountered at any moment, 56[*] different aspects of the three notes may be easily told off. These aspects exhibit not only the two superadded thirds and the fourth formed by the octave as already shown; but the sixth, octave and even the tenth, according to the

---

[*] This number is doubled when the chords are taken by the left hand.

omission of more or less notes. But the best way will be to proceed at once to detail them.

118. Obviously every chord must have the same number of positions as notes, seeing that each note in turn is liable to be placed highest or lowest. The natural position assumes the root to be in the bass; but, should the root be replaced in the bass by either of the other two notes, the combinations produced count as "inversions"—first and second respectively—the result being that a chord has one less inversion than it has notes. In inversions it is usual to leave out the actual bass note in the upper parts and to double some other, should fullness be required. At the same time this does not always happen; so that the simple ordinary dispositions of the triad notes exclusive of all positions beyond the octave amounts, say, to thirty-three, as shown in Ex. 131; and with the aspect of every one

Ex. 131

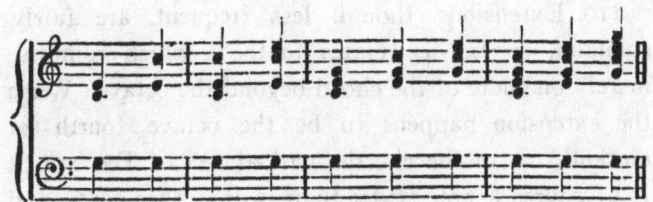

of these in every key, major and minor, the accompanist should be thoroughly familiar. In addition to this, the notes indicated in the example as being for the right hand should also be played by the left, whilst the right appropriates the present bass as melody; so that the real number of dispositions, without exceeding the octave, amounts to no less than sixty-six.

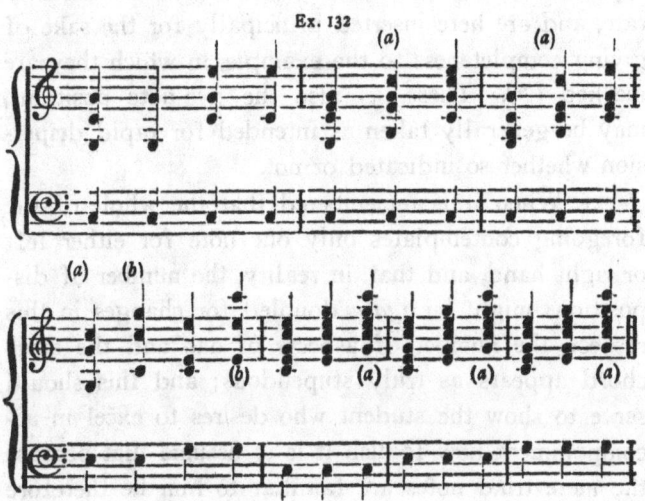

Ex. 132

119. Extensions, though less frequent, are fairly common, so far as relates to those which comprise merely one note of the chord beyond the octave. When the extension happens to be the octave fourth (or eleventh) as in the chords marked *(a)* of Ex. 132, it is of course a note wider than in the other cases, and correspondingly less frequent. Generally speaking, also, all positions are common in which the interval falling to the thumb and first finger is wide; from which it follows that several of the chords indicated may be difficult for the right hand whilst fairly easy for the left, and vice versa.

120. As for positions which extend to *two* notes of the chord beyond the octave, it is perhaps needless to say that, in accompaniment at least, they are extremely rare, and are here inserted principally for the sake of giving completeness to the example, in which they are marked *(b)*. These, as also the five-note positions, may be generally taken as intended for rapid dispersion whether so indicated or not.

121. When it is remembered that the whole of the foregoing contemplates only one note for either left or right hand, and that, in reality, the number of dispositions might be *again* doubled for changes in this respect, the number of aspects of one and the same chord appears as truly stupendous; and this should serve to show the student who desires to excel in accompaniment how foolish it is to assume that because the mere triad notes are familiar to him he therefore

Triad Positions Required in Accompaniment. 169

knows all that is necessary. At the same time no one would expect him to practise the triads fully in all these possible dispositions. What he is really wanted to do is to study their salient outward features until he is competent to recognise them quickly; and this he will never succeed in without learning to guage intervals with the eye. Thus, the second (with a side contact as outward sign) is typical of all the even numbers; or, in other words, of those intervals the note-heads of which are upon line and space. The third similarly represents intervals whose note-heads are both upon lines or spaces; as in the following example:

Ex. 133.

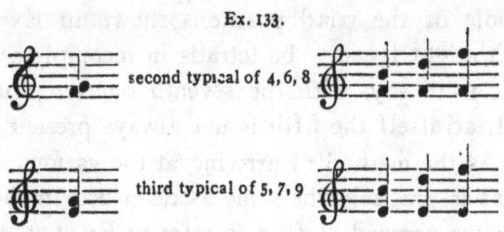

122. The word typical is here used only with regard to visible aspect; and, in reading, the eye requires to be trained to the amount of stave-space consisting of the intervention of one or more lines between the note-heads. There could be no greater folly than to grudge a little painstaking in this matter, the beneficial effect of proficiency in which is a constant and pleasant experience to the accompanist.

CHAPTER XVIII.

TETRAD POSITIONS REQUIRED IN ACCOMPANIMENT.

123. IT is but a natural step to apply what has just been said to the tetrad, or chord of four notes consisting of three thirds above a bass. To begin with, the whole of the triad positions shown in Exs. 131 and 132 might feasibly be tetrads in incomplete form, or, that is to say, with the seventh omitted; just as in the triad itself the fifth is not always present.

124. As the method of arriving at the various tetrad positions is precisely the same as described in the last chapter, we proceed at once to refer to Ex. 134; which

Ex. 134
Tetrad positions within the octave and with root bass

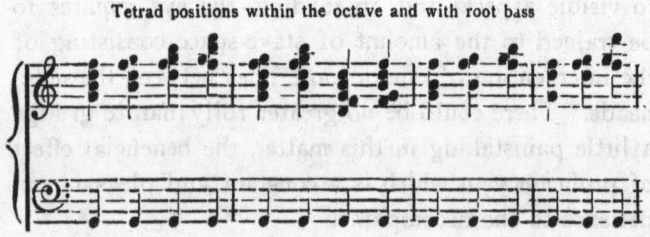

Tetrad Positions Required in Accompaniment. 171

consists of various arrangements of the dominant tetrad, within the octave, and with root bass. The aspect of this chord has a very marked feature in the side contact of two note-heads resulting from the inverted seventh. The upper of these two note-heads is the root—a fact well worth remembering in transposition—and the side-contact appears in all but the first position.

125. In Exs. 135, 136 and 137 we have tetrad positions in first, second and third inversions respectively. The chords marked *, though liable to be tetrads according to context, have (as far as mere notes is concerned) the appearance of being triads only. All chords in incomplete form are liable to alternate readings, the decision as to their real meaning depending upon the sense of the composition.

Ex 135.

Tetrad (first inversion).

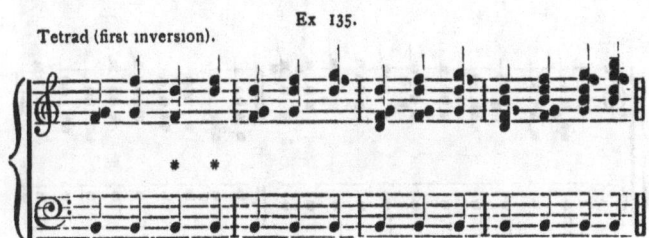

Tetrad (second inversion). Ex. 136

Tetrad (third inversion) Ex. 137

Ex. 138

Tetrad Positions Required in Accompaniment. 173

126. The chord selected for these examples is the dominant tetrad, consisting of major triad and minor seventh. It is the most usual and useful form; and, as such, is recommended to the student for the formation of figurations in conjunction with the triad. There is of course no limit to the designs which may be formed in this way, and the accompanist will find himself continually encountering fresh graceful forms based upon the same material. To treat this matter exhaustively is therefore quite out of question, and the examples are merely offered as elementary and suggestive. Ex. 139 is the alternation of dominant and tonic with occasional use of inversions in plain arpeggio In Ex. 140 the same form is purposely preserved; in order that the student may more easily learn

Ex. 139.

174 *How to Accompany.*

Tetrad Positions Required in Accompaniment. 175

to vary the upper notes, whilst remaining entirely within the chord. This condition is abandoned in Ex. 141; use being there made of the underchanging note, as indicated at *. At each of these places the note employed, though not within the harmony, is always exactly a semitone below it, and thus stands to it in the light of a melodic inflection. This will serve as a slight introduction to the chromatic changes with which we shall shortly have more freely to deal.

127. There are, in all, five tetrads, but they present enormous differences in their importance to the accompanist; and the following example, exhibiting the complete series, formed respectively of:

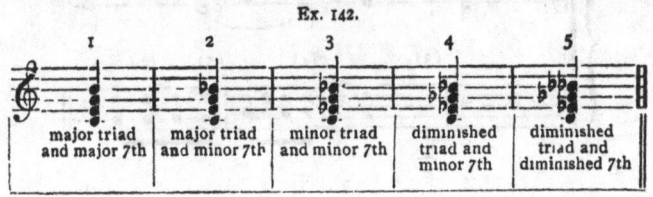

Ex. 142.

1	2	3	4	5
major triad and major 7th	major triad and minor 7th	minor triad and minor 7th	diminished triad and minor 7th	diminished triad and diminished 7th

will show the exact position occupied by each. No. 1 is the widest formation and also the least employed; the two referred to above as most useful to the accompanist being Nos. 2 and 5; or, the dominant and diminished tetrads, respectively. Both of these chords figure very largely as modulative agencies, and a special chapter will be devoted to each on that account; so that we are dispensed for the moment from enlarging upon that question The aspect of all tetrads in notation is precisely the same, and it is a simple question of musicianship whether the accompanist is able to detect to which of the above series each chord belongs. He is strongly advised to fix them in his mind whenever encountered and not to be satisfied with a mere reading of the notes—this being another habit most favourable to facility in transposition. To illustrate the whole matter would require a voluminous amount of example, but this should not be necessary for an attentive reader; as Ex. 143 ex-

hibits fairly and once for all how these chords are liable to occur. Here, within the short space of two bars, we have no less than four different kinds of tetrads; in fact, all of them except the major. They may easily be identified by comparing the indicated numbers with those of Ex. 142, and keen observation should be made of the manner of passing from one tetrad to another by mere semitonal change in one of the parts. Thus, when stripped of all ornamentation,

Tetrad Positions Required in Accompaniment. 177

the progression of chords in Ex. 143 amounts simply to the following:

Herein, No. 3, on F, passes to No. 2, on D, by the mere change of one of the parts from E flat to D; No. 2, on D, passes to No. 5, on B, by a similar fall from C to B; and No. 5, on B, passes to G dominant by the melody falling from A flat to G. The student must regard it as indispensable always to know what particular tetrad results from changes such as above indicated; the grand point being that these matters are the same no matter in what key he may be required to play his accompaniment.

CHAPTER XIX.

THE DOMINANT SEVENTH IN MODULATION.

128. THE most natural application of the dominant seventh as a modulative agency is in going round the circle of keys, and especially in making the journey by successive *sub*dominants; because, in that way, each chord stands in the relation of dominant to the next key, and requires only the addition of a minor seventh to the triad to make the harmony complete. This progression is therefore selected for our first example; and, in order to accustom the student at once to figurations in which chromatic changes occur, so that his grasp of the prevailing harmony may not be disturbed by their presence, the "under-changing note" is introduced, in Ex. 144, in the same way as has already been done in Ex. 141. It will be observed that, in Ex 144, each bar represents one key, to the dominant and tonic of which the two halves of the bar are respectively given. It therefore follows that the same root-bass falls to the second half of one bar as to the first of the next; first in triad, and next in tetrad form—

The Dominant Seventh in Modulation.

Ex. 144.

the latter being the result of adding the minor seventh, so as to completely govern the coming key. The flow of keys by this progression is so natural, however, that it is not even positively necessary to add the dominant seventh in every case. Thus, it would be quite permissible to assume each alternate chord to be a dominant without staying to repeat it as a full tetrad; and by this means to effect a modulation round the entire circle of keys in exactly half the time, as shown in Ex. 145. In such cases the addition of the

Ex 145.

seventh does no more than make the modulation more assertive; for we have already seen, in Exs. 52 and 55 (major) and 120 and 122 (minor), that it is possible to travel round the keys with triads alone. It follows, therefore, that, although the added seventh may give extra power to these modulations, its real utility as a modulative agency consists in effecting the passage between keys which are more distantly removed.

129. Nothing is easier than to obtain a complete grasp of this means of modulation, as it simply depends upon there being a note in common between the tonic-triad we are quitting and the dominant of the new key. Accordingly, in Ex 146, each note of the chord of C is shown to be common to four dominant chords. These do not count for twelve modulations, however, as the three marked *(a)* and the two

Ex. 146.

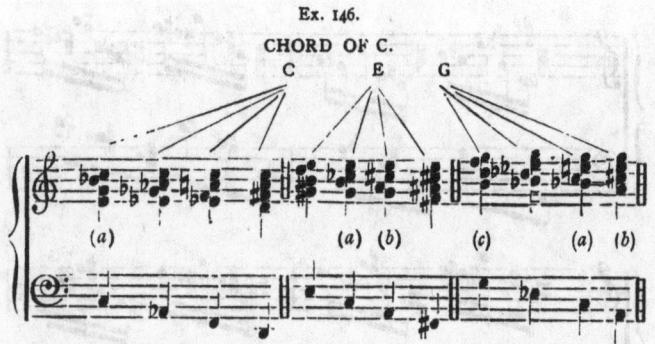

marked *(b)* are the same; whilst that marked *(c)* is no modulation at all, on account of leading back to the original key. These exceptions amount of a deduction of four from the twelve; after allowing for which there remain (in immediate sequel to the triad of any key) eight modulations open to the dominant chord; those namely from C to

$\overset{1}{\text{C}\sharp}$ or D♭; $\overset{3}{\text{D}\natural}$; $\overset{4}{\text{F}}$; $\overset{5}{\text{G}}$; $\overset{6}{\text{A}♭}$; $\overset{7}{\text{A}\natural}$; B♭ and $\overset{8}{\text{B}\natural}$;

or, of course, from any key whatever to another key situated at:

1. A minor second above (or major seventh below)
2. A major second above (or minor seventh below).
3. A perfect fourth above (or perfect fifth below)
4. A perfect fifth above (or perfect fourth below).
5. A minor sixth above (or major third below).
6. A major sixth above (or minor third below).
7. A minor seventh above (or major second below).
8. A major seventh above (or minor second below).

The Dominant Seventh in Modulation. 183

130. It will be our purpose to exhibit these modulations in the interesting form of being provided with figurations of a kind which the accompanist is likely to encounter in actual work; but, as No. 3 has been already illustrated by Ex. 144, and No. 7 by Ex. 145, the samples now to be given consist of Nos. 1, 2, 4, 5, 6 and 8 of the above series.

131. Ex. 147 is an instance of modulation to the minor second (semitone) above; and is No. 1 of the above series. It must be carried through the keys, but need only be commenced from C; for, on account of proceeding by semitones, it comprises every key by the mere process of returning to C.

184 *How to Accompany.*

132. Ex. 148 is a modulation to the perfect fifth above (or fourth below) being No. 4 of the series. It need only be carried from C to C once; as, proceeding by fifths, it comprises the whole circle of keys.

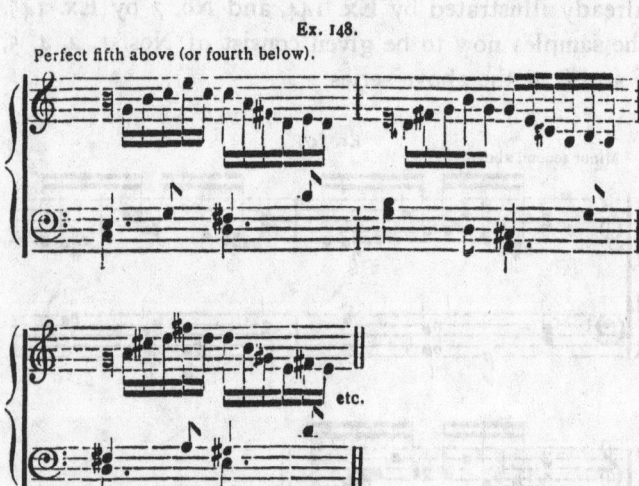

Ex. 148.
Perfect fifth above (or fourth below).

133. Ex. 149 is a modulation to the minor third below (or major sixth above) being No. 6 of the series. This must be started from three successive semitones; returning to the starting-point in each case, in order to render the series of required modulations complete. Thus:

C to A; A to G♭; G♭ to E♭; E♭ to C.
D♭ to B♭; B♭ to G; G to E; E to D♭.
D to B; B to A♭; A♭ to F; F to D.

The Dominant Seventh in Modulation.

Ex. 149.

Minor third below

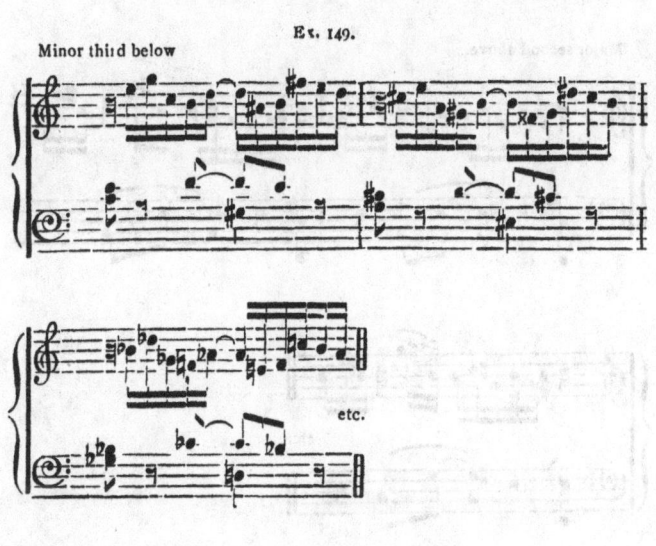

Ex. 150

Major second above.

Ex 151.

Major second above.

etc.

134. Exs. 150 and 151 are both samples of modulation to the major second above; being illustrations of No. 2 of the series. They must be started from two successive semitones returning as before to each starting point; thus:

C to D; D to E; E to F♯ or G♭; G♭ to A♭; A♭ to B♭; B♭ to C.

D♭ to E♭; E♭ to F; F to G; G to A; A to B; B to C♯ or D♭.

135. Ex. 152 exhibits modulation to the minor second (semitone) below (or major seventh above) and is No. 8 of the series. It need only be carried from C to C; for the same reason as in the case of Ex. 147.

The Dominant Seventh in Modulation. 187

Ex. 152.
Minor second below.

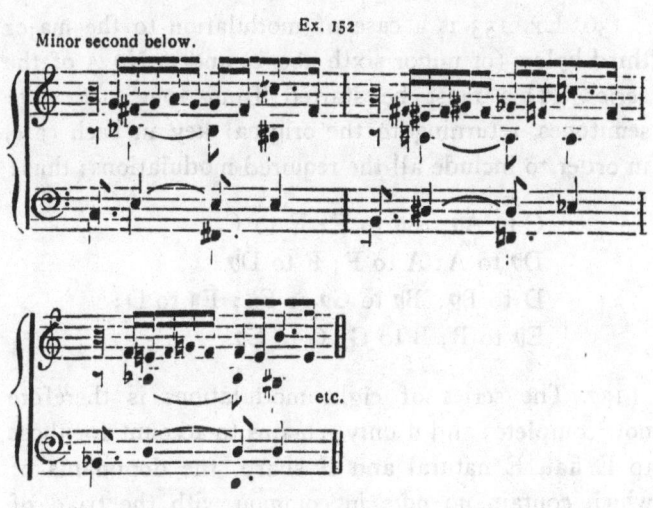

etc.

Ex. 153.
Major third below.

136. Ex. 153 is a case of modulation to the major third below (or minor sixth above) and is No 5 of the series. This must be started from four successive semitones, returning to the original key in each case, in order to include all the required modulations; thus :

>C to A♭; A♭ to E; E to C.
>D♭ to A; A to F; F to D♭.
>D to B♭; B♭ to G♭ or F♯; F♯ to D;
>E♭ to B; B to G; G to E♭.

137. The series of eight modulations is therefore now complete; and it only remains to account for those to E flat, E natural and F sharp, the dominants of which contain no note in common with the triad of C. In this connection it is to be observed that, although they contain nothing in common with the *tonic* chord of C, a link exists with the *dominant* of that key and that this link is what we shall now utilise for modulating purposes. Thus, if we take the notes of the chord of G dominant (with added ninth), then, by following the method pursued in the case of Ex. 146, and therefore treating them individually as connecting links with the key of C modulations to the remaining keys can be smoothly effected. It now only remains to give figurations of these after the same plan as that adopted for the series of eight; and although Ex. 154 appears to give six modulations there are only three in reality; for the reason that the dominant of C gives two connecting links in each case.

The Dominant Seventh in Modulation.

Ex. 154.

Thus to pass into E we have B and A;

To pass into F sharp we have B and E sharp (F natural);

To pass into E flat we have D and F;

as may be easily perceived from the above; and perhaps even still more easily and pleasantly from the ensuing illustrations Exs. 155 and 157 exhibit modulations to the augmented fourth above; and, as this modulation divides the octave equally, it must be taken from six starting points before the exercise is complete. Thus:

                C to F♯ or G♭; G♭ to C.
                D♭ to G; G to D♭.
                D to A♭; A♭ to D.
                E♭ to A; A to E♭.
                E to B♭; B♭ to E.
                F to B: B to F

How to Accompany

Ex. 155.
Augmented fourth or diminished fifth, above or below

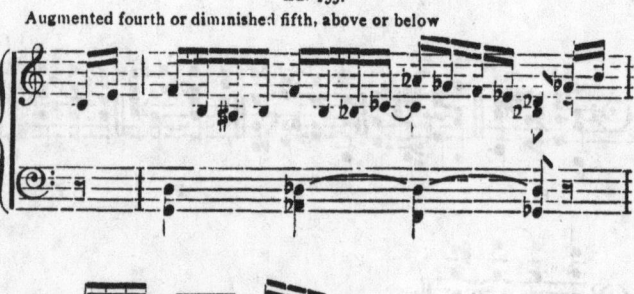

Ex. 157

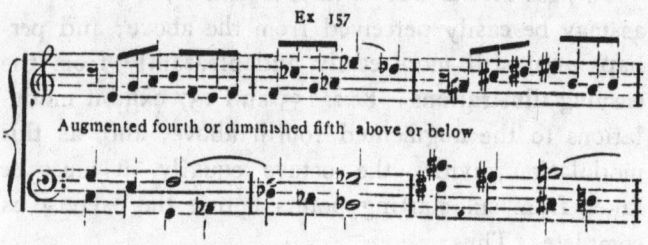

Augmented fourth or diminished fifth above or below

The Dominant Seventh in Modulation.

138. Ex. 156 shows the modulation to a major third above, and must be taken from four starting points to make it complete; thus:

    C to E; E to A♮; A♭ to C.
    D♭ to F; F to A; A to D♭.
    D to F♯ or G♭; G♭ to B♮; B♭ to D.
    E♭ to G; G to B; B to E♭.

Ex. 156.
Major third above

139. Ex. 158 is a sample of modulation to the minor third above, requiring to be completed as under:

    C to E♭; E♭ to F♯; F♯ to A; A to C.
    D♭ to E; E to G; G to B♭; B♭ to D♭.
    D to F; F to A♭; A♭ to B; B to D.

192   *How to Accompany.*

Ex. 158.

These exercises, properly carried out, constitute a full school for the accompanist in this means of modulation. They unfailingly result in an increased general facility besides greatly favouring the act of transposition.

CHAPTER XX.

THE DIMINISHED SEVENTH IN MODULATION

140. OF all chords employed in modulative progressions that of the diminished seventh is most in request; and, as we are at present concerned only with its practical utility in this respect, we shall not trouble about enharmonics, but regard this chord as simply dividing the octave into four minor thirds; subject of course to the understanding that one of them must be represented enharmonically in notation by the augmented second. By looking at the matter from this purely mechanical standpoint the accompanist is enabled to confine his attention to *three chords*; as, by taking a fourth, he would merely arrive at a second position of the first. Thus:

The differing notation of these chords is entirely a question of the position of the augmented second, as already stated. Thus, in the above example, it is placed in:

No. 1. Between E♮ and F♯.
No. 2. Between B♮ and C♯.
No. 3. Between A♮ and B♮;

but, on the other hand, the very same chords from the accompanist's point of view might have presented quite a different aspect. The context of the composition might, for example, have required them to be written as under:

Ex. 159a.

in which case the augmented seconds would have fallen, respectively, to B double flat, C; G, A sharp and C flat, D. The theoretical reasons which underlie these differences are not our present concern, which is strictly that of the *modulative power* of these three combinations, irrespective of the manner of their description. This power is truly immense; as the mere striking of one of these chords upon the keyboard enables the player to pass at once into any key whatever. This will be found graphically exhibited in Ex. 160, where a cadence into every key is braced against each one of the chords in turn.

The Diminished Seventh in Modulation.

Ex. 160.

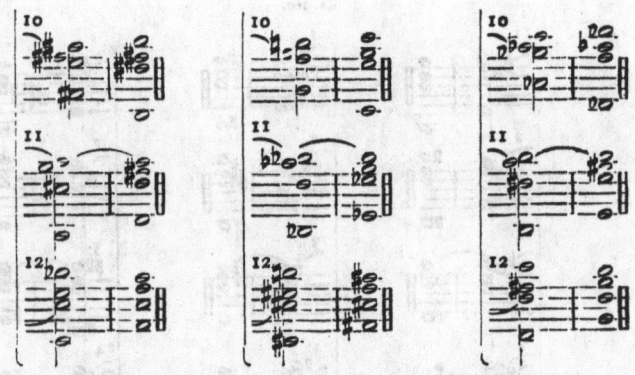

141. It is of course one thing to play these and quite another to understand how the modulations are effected. Mere performance will be of slight benefit to the accompanist, whose art depends far more upon musicianship than execution. We will therefore proceed to dissect the matter for his guidance.

142. The diminished seventh has the faculty of passing at once into the key of any of its notes. This accounts for cadences 5, 6, 7, 8 of Ex. 160. It also has the faculty of adopting any of its notes as the dominant of a new key. This accounts for cadences 9, 10, 11 and 12 of the same example. There are therefore only four keys remaining to provide for in order to complete the circle of twelve; and this is accomplished with equal facility though requiring a slight illustration. The process consists simply of regarding the note lying nearest the dominant of the key into which we wish to pass as a suspension. It follows then that

The Diminished Seventh in Modulation. 197

by causing the note in question to fall a semitone we are merely resolving a suspension. But it so happens that by that resolution we are providing ourselves with just the four missing dominants required to complete the circle of keys. If we select the first column of Ex. 160 as a case in point we find the diminished seventh chord to be either F sharp, A, C, E flat; or, the same notes upon the keyboard, in enharmonic equivalents. We have already passed from this chord into:

F♯ \
A } by adopting each of its notes as tonic of a
C }   new key;
E /

and also into:

B \
D } by adopting each of its notes as dominant of
F }   a new key;
A♭ /

so that the only keys remaining are those of D flat, E, G and B flat, the dominants of which are respectively A flat, B, D and F. As these notes are to become the resolutions of suspensions it follows that:

A flat is suspended by B double flat (enharmonic equivalent of A); *see Ex. 161 (a);*

F is suspended by G flat (enharmonic equivalent of F sharp); *see Ex. 161 (b);*

D is suspended by E flat; *see Ex. 161 (c);*

B is suspended by C; *see Ex. 161 (d);*

How to Accompany.

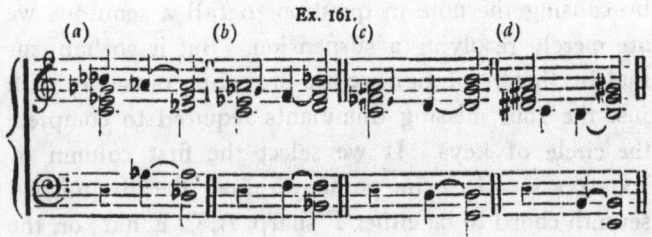

Ex. 161.

and accordingly we pass quite naturally into the four remaining keys of D flat, E, G and B flat, and the whole range of tonalities is complete and governed by the one chord. The reader should not hold this to be a light privilege because it is arrived at so easily; the fact being that it is the momentary disregard of enharmonics which enables him to condense this matter for practical use. He has still to accustom himself to the varied aspects of the three diminished seventh chords in notation; but that is also now much simplified, because, by the light of what has been said, he knows that in reading one note of the chord the others follow as a matter of course.

143. It would certainly be most interesting and form a delightful collection of studies to give figurations of all these modulations after the same plan as that adopted in the case of the dominant seventh But it will be obvious to the reader that this would afford ample matter for a separate volume and that it is on that account impossible in course of the present work to give him more than an indication of the way in

The Diminished Seventh in Modulation. 199

which composers are liable to apply this means. Ex. 162 consists of two passages, both commencing in the

Ex. 162

same way and both consisting of the same melodic outline; yet one of them as naturally concludes in the key of G as the other does in that of D flat. A player who is conversant with what has just been explained will see at once that in the first passage the E flat of the diminished seventh falls to D as dominant of G whereas in the second it is A which falls to A flat as dominant of D flat. It follows too that the same natural character and the same melodic outline might have been equally well preserved to pass into any other key.

144. It will now be necessary to say something of the various positions which this chord is liable to assume. The most practical forms will be found detailed in Ex. 163; from which it will be seen that the

Ex. 163.

chord is highly favourable to a full harmony, as it enables a five-note combination to be given without exceeding the octave in compass. Even the tenth positions are easier than those of the triads; because the tenth is always minor, and therefore a semitone less in stretch of the hand. There should be no difficulty experienced in becoming familiar with all these positions and even in applying to them some elementary

The Diminished Seventh in Modulation. 201

form of figuration for practice sake. Moreover, as there are, mechanically considered, only three such chords, the whole might easily be practised in the same way, and a new facility in accompaniment thus acquired without much trouble. The student should have no difficulty in finding forms to make this application, as, even in the event of his being unable to invent them for himself he will find an abundance of patterns to select from in the examples given throughout this book. After he has become proficient in forms which consist of mere dispersion of the harmony he will find it improving to apply the underchanging note as in Ex. 141. This, however, is admittedly difficult; and, being so, is recommended rather as a counsel of perfection to the enthusiast than as advice to the ordinary reader.

CHAPTER XXI.

CHROMATIC MODULATION.

145. THE subject of chromatic modulation is so vast that, in order to ensure an absolute clearness, it will be best, considering the limited space at our disposal, to focus all the instruction to be given upon one typical case. By this method we shall be enabled, without going beyond our limit, to show how one and the same theme can by chromatic modulation be made subject to almost endless variety of treatment, and how in accompaniment a complete change of aspect is often associated with the same material.

146. Chromatic modulations are mostly liable to appear as climax is approached, and may therefore, in the general sense, be said to tend in that direction. The accompanist should always make a point of knowing the moment of greatest passion or excitement, as graduations of touch are much influenced thereby. We will therefore begin by adopting Ex. 164 as the climax

Chromatic Modulation.

Ex. 164.

of what we are about to illustrate, and towards which the various chromatic modulative passages exhibited have a natural inclination to lead.

Ex. 165.

147. In course of developing this idea the simple passage of Ex. 165 is offered as showing the chromatic division of small melodic intervals. The great feature about chromatics is that, as the semitone is the smallest interval of our twelve-semitone octave, it is neutral, in the sense of not being identified with any tonality.

The result is that it does not necessarily modulate; and, in Ex. 165, its application is purposely of the most innocent description. But we have only to imagine the same form of accompaniment to be approaching a re-entry of the theme and the uses of chromatic change become at once apparent; showing as they do the difference between modulations effected in this way and those which are the result of calculated chord-successions An illustration of this is afforded by Ex. 166; which, starting in C, passes through the keys of F, D flat, F sharp, B and G, finally bursting with éclat upon the key of C, all in the course of four bars, and without giving sufficient time to allow of any effect of incoherence.

148. An episode of this description betokens the approaching end of a song on account of the return to the theme being in the original key. Let us now therefore suppose the accompaniment to relate to some middle phase of the piece, in which the return to the theme is made principally for the sake of unity; and not, therefore, as indicating anything in the way of approaching conclusion. This is exhibited in Ex. 167 in which the chromatics take us transiently through a variety of keys (each of which the accompanist should distinctly realise notwithstanding subordinate position in the phrase) finally emerging upon the key of D, which of course could just as easily have been any other key according to the desire of the composer.

Chromatic Modulation.

205

Ex. 165.

Ex. 167.

206   How to Accompany.

149 All these examples have such intensity of expression that there might be some danger of the student supposing chromatic modulation to be always subject to this association; but, as a matter of fact, it lies in wait for the accompanist equally in meditative and plaintive episodes. This especially applies to ultra-modern music, which very often seems to be based rather upon the chromatic than upon any diatonic scale; and an experienced accompanist knows, by the style of work in hand, the amount of chromatic modulation which he may fairly expect

150 By way of illustration therefore we will now apply the same figure to a meditative passage. This is shown in Ex. 168; and the very fact of quietude

Chromatic Modulation.

Ex. 168.

renders this accompaniment difficult to play on account of the absolute equality of touch required. To disturb this would be to break the continuity from which the whole effect is derived. Yet the outward aspect of the passage is very much the same as before; which will serve to show how a good accompaniment depends even more upon the player's knowledge than upon his mechanical skill.

Chromatic Modulation.

151. The last example, however, by no means represents an extreme; for, by transference to the bass, the same figure may be made to contribute to an effect so despondent as finally to die away into silence. This is only another way of stating that there is no limit to its application, so that one more illustration must now suffice. In Ex. 169 we have a despondent form of the same figure, stated simply; and, in Ex. 170, by

way of showing the easy manipulation of chromatic means, this despondency is allowed to revive and to return to the theme with exultation. There are those who regard these chromaticisms of modern music as extremely clever, but the truth lies all the other way. They form a most valuable means, but are so easy to manage that there could be no greater sign of weakness than their frequent employment. With that frequent (and indeed sometimes incessant) employment the accompanist must needs reckon, however, and it is for that reason that in the present work the subject of chromatic modulation has been deemed worthy of separate treatment.

CHAPTER XXII

TRANSPOSITION.

152. TRANSPOSITION would not be so difficult if players were more generally familiar with the use of the C clefs. But even better than the habit of any special clef is that of *reading intervals* rather than notes. The fact is often lost sight of that clefs are not intended to indicate a fixed name for individual notes, but that these names merely result from the interval which separates the notes which bear them from the standard. The habit of reading intervals is therefore at all times the correct one; and it is only the prevalent use of certain clefs in particular which has caused it to be supplanted by that of regarding certain positions upon the stave as being specially associated with individual notes.

153. In course of these pages there have been so many allusions to the question of transposition, so many helps suggested, and so many exercises given with a view to facilitate it (to say nothing of the staple

method of working all figurations round the circle of keys) that the student who has conscientiously followed the instruction thus far can scarcely be expected to experience much difficulty. For all that, however, we will take things as they are, and treat the question quite from the ordinary standpoint.

154. The easiest transposition is from any key to some other bearing the same letter. Every key, either major or minor, which bears the name of a natural note is liable to this transposition either upwards or downwards; and in the case of the natural major or minor keys to both Thus C major and A minor may have to be transposed into C sharp or C flat or into A sharp or A flat minor respectively. These keys with seven sharps or flats are not in ordinary use nowadays; but the accompanist who has to transpose will always find it easier to use the same letter for the new key if possible, and therefore to prefer to think of C sharp when transposing from C—even although the same piece written out might be easier to read in D flat.

155. Of all the other major keys F is alone liable to be *raised* (to F sharp), the remainder being subject only to be *lowered*; as:

A to A flat (A sharp not in use).
B to B flat (B sharp not in use)
D to D flat (D sharp not in use)
E to E flat (E sharp not in use).
G to G flat (G sharp not in use).

On the other hand the minor keys are all liable to be raised; except:

E to E flat (E sharp not in use).

B to B flat (B sharp not in use).

156. Transpositions of this kind involve not only the mental adoption of a new key-signature, but the mental addition to, and subtraction from, all accidentals. This is so embarrassing *without*, and yet so easy *with* a little practice, that it is astonishing to find those often called upon to accompany seldom making it the object of any methodical painstaking. And here it will become evident to the reader why we have devoted so much pains to the subject of modulation; for this mental addition and subtraction of accidentals ceases on the instant of the key changing to one which does not admit of retention of the same letter. Let us suppose, for example, that, in a simple piece requiring to be transposed from F to F sharp, the passage occurred marked *(a)* in Ex. 171. This

Ex. 171.

would offer not the slightest difficulty as the signature of six sharps renders it a case of ordinary reading. But suppose the piece to have modulated, and the same passage to recur as at *(b)* in the same example, not only the six-sharp signature would be rendered useless, but the mental conversion of sharps into double sharps would be frightfully cumbersome, even if possible. As a matter of fact it would not be practicable at all, on account of landing us upon an impossible E double sharp; whereas the player should simply recognise the modulation which has taken place, and, knowing the key of F sharp not to be capable of being raised without change of letter, change the letter mentally accordingly. It follows therefore that, although the transposition into a key bearing the same letter is a question only of key-signature and accidentals, that only applies while the modulations of the piece permit. The mere fore-knowledge of this circumstance is a protection in itself.

157. The student will see therefore that facility in modulation counts for a great deal in transposition because the quick recognition of modulation is always necessary in order to change the mental process to suit the circumstances. We now pass on to transpositions of the second above or below, but in this, as in all other transpositions, precepts only apply whilst the composition remains in keys closely related to that in which it started. The following table may be use-

ful as exhibiting all possible transpositions of the second:

Ex 172.

	Transposition o second below.	Original Key	Transposition to second above.
Major Keys	B* or B♭	C♮, C♯ or C♭	D or D♭*
	A or A♭	B or B♭	C, C♯ or C♭*
	G or G♭	A or A♭	B or B♭
	F or F♯*	G or G♭	A or A♭
	E or E♭	F or F♯	G or G♭*
	D or D♭	E or E♭	F or F♯
	C or C♭	D or D♭	E or E♭
Minor Keys	G or G♯*	A♮, A♯ or A♭	B or B♭*
	F or F♯	G or G♯	A, A♯ or A♭*
	E or E♭	F or F♯	G or G♯
	D or D♯*	E or E♭	F or F♯
	C or C♯	D or D♯	E or E♭*
	B or B♭	C or C♯	D or D♯
	A, A♯* or A♭	B or B♭	C or C♯

158. The transpositions marked * are possible enharmonic changes, included necessarily in a tabular exposition; the rest being changes of either one, two, or three semitones upwards or downwards, without change of letter in the key-note. The information contained in the above is so familiar that it is contemptuously treated as a rule, with the result that it is not ready for instant application. The prudent student will not be too proud to take note of the range of this kind of transposition.

159. With regard to the mere finding of notes in the new key so much may be conceded in favour of habit in individual cases that whatever may be said is liable to modification in that respect. But it is quite easy to deliver judgment upon this question in the abstract; and, therefore, to advise students whose habits are not yet formed, or, at all events, have not become inveterate. All such may rely that the perfect method of reading the note-heads is by the intervals between them irrespective of names. The same applies to chords, the various intervals composing which contribute to give different aspects to different combinations —a subject which has already been copiously alluded to. Everything which holds fast to the inherent contents of the composition and is neutral as to tonality favours transposition. It has already been shown how useful it is to follow the course of modulation in order to change the mental process quickly when necessary, but independently of that it is useful; as, in a chain of chords, each one gives a clue to the identity of the next. This explains why it is easier to transpose a good composition than a bad one; because in the latter there is little or no *meaning* to transpose, whereas in a good work context is a wonderful assistance.

160. The only remaining transpositions are those in the third and fourth above or below. There is obviously no transposition beyond the fourth, for the reason that the fifth is the fourth inverted, the sixth the third, the seventh the second and the octave the

unison. It will also be unnecessary to tabularise these transpositions, as the keys in question remain as in Ex. 172; besides which the same table which give the second will also give the third or fourth by merely reading a line up or down to suit the occasion.

161. Mechanically speaking, the most difficult transposition is the fourth, not only because it is the widest interval but also because the note heads of the new key fall, as to lines and spaces, upon the opposite of the original. It is true that this may be avoided by reading a fifth the other way, but this is a remedy worse than the evil, on account of the width of the interval. It is however consoling for the legitimate student to reflect that these troubles only arise as a consequence of not reading intervals only, in which case the transposition of a fourth is rather easier than the others on account of the close relationship of the keys involved.

162. In closing this subject, and by way of a parting word to the earnest student, we would say:

"Make sure of a facility in transposing the *augmented* fourth, and all the others will appear easy."

---

163. The moment has now arrived for bidding adieu alike to the reader and to this fascinating subject. Much indeed remains to be said upon it which limitation of space has compelled us to forego; but it may perhaps be permitted to us to indulge the aspiration

that what *has* been said will prove to be of some benefit; and perhaps not only to accompanists, for whose help it is directly intended, but indirectly to the wider class interested in the various questions of musicianship incidentally treated

GENERAL INDEX

GENERAL INDEX.

(The Numbers Refer to Paragraphs except in the Case of Examples.)

A

Accent in alternations . . . . Ex. 108
Accentuation (amount of to be ascertained from formation of the group) 63
——— in semiquaver groups (when at minimum) . . 63
Accidentals, addition to and subtraction from in transposition 156
Accompaniment (differences from solo playing) 70, 141
——— (primitive purpose of) 3
——— (purely subordinate and otherwise) 62
——— (tabular exposition of styles of) . . . . . Ex. 11
——— (unison) . . . . Ex. 1
Accompanist's simultaneous reading of voice part specially desirable in polyphony 48
Act of transposition 159
Agitato by fragmentary tremolo . . . . Ex. 89
Alternate readings of incomplete chords 125
——— single and double notes in accompaniment
73, Ex. 82, Ex. 85
Alternation (a means of increased brilliancy) . . . 89
——— (a means of lightness) . . . . Ex. 101-2
——— (a means of quicker motion) 87
——— (a neutral means, applicable to varieties of effect) . 88
——— (in accompaniment, with special designs) Ex. 105-6
——— (independently in accompaniment) . Ex. 103
——— (in elaboration of unison effects) 88

How to Accompany.

Alternation (in harmonic progression against voice) 88, Ex. 104
——— (of equal numbers) . . . . . 90, Ex. 94-5, Ex. 107
Alternations arising from mechanical necessity 92
——— of equal numbers with unequal time . . . 91, Ex. 109
——— (varieties of) 86
Alto of accompaniment (melody in) . . . . 44, Ex. 44, Ex. 47
——— part evolved from accompaniment . . . . 64, Ex. 79
Antique character of polyphonic accompaniment 51
Arpeggio (a means of lightening the chord repetition) . . 8
——— (as adaptation of the "phrase chord") 21
——— (as type of figuration) . . . . Ex. 6
——— (extended ostinato motive) . . . . . . 66, Ex. 80
——— (most usual means of figuration) 60
Ascending and descending dispersion of chords . . . 60, 62
Aspects of the triad in notation (various) . . . 117, 121
Augmented second of diminished seventh chord . . . 140
——— second (of harmonic minor scale) 113

B.

Band-score (accompaniments arranged from) 23
Bass of accompaniment in treble register . . . 46, Ex. 46
——— of accompaniment (melody in) . . . . . 9, Ex. 7
——— of accompaniment (melody in) not favoured by
    good composers 41
——— rhythmic figures 33
Brahms later piano works for cultivation of accompani-
    ments with melody in alto 44
Broken chords 69, 93c

C.

Cadence by diminished seventh into all keys . . . . Ex. 160
Cadences . . . . Ex. 54, Ex. 56, Ex. 121, Ex. 123
Characteristic figure (further example of) . . . . Ex. 127
——— figure (minor) carried through all the keys and in
    all positions . . . . Ex. 124-6
——— figure (with major dominants) . . . . . . Ex. 128
——— ostinato figure 99-100, 116
——— ostinato (simplest form) . . . . Ex. 115

General Index.   223

Characteristic ostinato with passing notes	Ex. 116-7
Chorale	6
Choral music (accompaniment of, its special character)	52
Chord and arpeggio combined in accompaniment	69
———-progressions	Ex. 53
———-repetitions in cross-rhythms	85
———-repetitions in cross-rhythms (illustrated)	Ex. 99a-100
———-repetitions with syncopation	Ex. 99
Chords (repeated, as form of accompaniment)	7-8, 33, 35
Chromatic modulation (illustration of)	Ex. 165-70
——— scale as basis	149
Church music (unison accompaniment in)	3
Clefs (familiarity with various)	152
Climax	105, Ex. 164
"Concertante" accompaniment	13, 39
Contrasting features of ostinato figures	103, 104
Counter-melody	11, 13
Counterpoint	9, 12, 48
Crescendo effects in accompaniment	72, Ex. 84

D.

Descending dispersions (tendency of, to evolve separate melody)	62
Dialogue with voice (bass of accompaniment in)	42
Diminished seventh cadenced into all keys	Ex. 160
——— seventh (illustration of use of suspensions in modulation)	Ex. 162
——— seventh (notation of)	Ex. 159a, Ex. 161
——— seventh (positions of)	144, Ex. 159, Ex. 163
Dispersion by arpeggio as elementary figuration	60, 93c
——— (hand-alternation one form of)	86
——— (of extended positions)	59
Dominant (in relation to the circle of keys)	55-6
——— (major in minor keys)	108
——— (retention of, as fifth in tonic chord a familiar form of holding-note)	36, Ex. 33
——— seventh in progression round circle of keys	128
Dominants (successive), Progression of triads by	Ex. 52

How to Accompany.

Dominant tetrad (various positions of) 126
Double and single notes in alternation 69-70
─── note accompaniment (combining chord and arpeggio)
  Ex. 81
─── notes including melody in left hand 45
─── notes of accompaniment (simultaneous with melody)
  73, Ex. 86
Doubling of the melody in triad dispersions . . . . Ex. 71
Duet with the voice (a result of ostinato figures) 94

E.

Enharmonics 140, 142, 158
Evolution of inner melody in triad dispersion . . . Ex. 67
─── of inner melody in triad dispersion (exercise on by successive dominants) . . . . Ex. 68
─── of inner melody in triad dispersion (exercise on by successive subdominants) . . . . Ex. 69
─── of separate melody in accompaniment . . . 62, Ex. 66
Exercise (showing method of using circle of keys for figuration) . . . . Ex. 72-3
Extended positions (figuration with chromatics) . . Ex. 141
─── positions (figuration within the harmony) . . Ex. 140
─── positions of the tetrad . . . . Ex. 138
─── positions of the triad . 59, 114, 119-20, Ex. 59, Ex. 132
─── positions (simple dispersion) . . . . Ex. 139

F.

Fanfare effects (their connection with the holding-note) . . 38
Figuration 8, 9
─── (a treatment of already existing material) . . . 15
─── (elementary) . . . . Ex. 6
─── (its relation to the mechanics of accompaniment) . . 53
─── of the tetrad 126
Figurations (difference between those of solo work and vocal accompaniments) 14
Fingering (uniformity of, from ostinato motives) 65, 102, 106
Five-note positions of diminished seventh 144
───-note positions of the triad 120

General Index

Folk-song (unaccompanied) 3
Form . . . . , , , 9, 13
Formation of simple rhythmic figures . . . . . Ex. 110
Four semiquaver group 60, 63
——— semiquaver group (as representative of holding-note) . . . . Ex. 75
——— semiquaver group (in support of melody) . . Ex. 74
——— semiquaver group (with returning notes) . . Ex. 76
Fourth (upper note of, as indicating root of triad) 116, Ex. 130
Full cadences 58

G.

Groups (four-semiquaver) resulting from dispersion of triad octave positions 60, 63
——— (triplet) resulting from triad dispersion 60

H

Half-cadences . . . . Ex. 58
Hand-alternation . . . . 35, 86, 93c, Ex. 32
Harmonisation below the melody . . . . 5, 30, Ex. 3, Ex. 27
——— (plain, illustrated) , ... Ex. 26
——— (plain) . . . . 4, 29, Ex. 2
——— (plain, defined) 32
Harmony (change of during vocal sostenuto) . 27-8, Ex. 24-5
——— (characteristics of restful and changeful) 24
———, Resources of 10
——— (retention of same) . . . . Ex. 20-1
Holding-note 10, 36-40, 46, 93b
Holding-note as represented by reiterations in chord dispersion 62
———-note (in reiteration) . . . . Ex. 8, Ex. 34-8
———-note (in sostenuto) . . . . Ex. 33
———-note (periodical return to) . . . . Ex. 39
———-note (varied illustration of) . . . . . . Ex 40

I.

Identification of bass of accompaniment with voice part
                                                          43, Ex. 43
Increase in size of chord indicative of slight crescendo .   Ex. 83
Independent melodic progression, a feature of the characteristic figure 100
——— vocal part in polyphony 12, 48
Indeterminate number of parts in polyphonic accompaniment 50
Inner part of accompaniment (melody in) 9, 44
——— voice evolved from semiquaver groups 64
Instrumental effects in accompaniment 42
Interspersed symphonies 13, 22, 42
Intervals (the reading of) 121, 159
Inversions 118

L.

Legato sign (unreliable as an indication of phrasing) . . . 16
Lighter rhythmic figures 98
——— rhythmic figures (illustrated) . . . . . . Ex. 114
Light pulsations in chord repetition following a strong bass 83
——— pulsations in chord repetition (illustrated) . . Ex. 97-8

M.

Major keys (circle of) . . . . Ex. 51
——— triads (progression of, round the circle of keys, by successive subdominants) . . . . Ex. 55
——— triads (progression of, round the circle of keys, by successive dominants) . . . . Ex. 52
Material subject to figuration either rhythmical, melodic or harmonic 15
Melodic inflections against sustained accompaniment . Ex. 22
——— progressions evolved from chord-distribution . . . 62
Melodies (simple, most appropriate for plain harmonisation) 30
Melody 4, 5
——— (as bass of accompaniment) . . . 9, 41, 93b, Ex. 7
——— as bass of accompaniment (restricted use of) 42, Ex. 42
——— in alto of accompaniment 44

Melody in tenor of accompaniment . . . . . 44-5, Ex. 45
Method of working round the circle of keys 68, 114
Minor keys (circle of) . . . . 107, Ex. 119*a*
——— mode (want of sufficient familiarity with) . . . 114
——— ostinato figure carried out in full, in the three positions of the triad . . . . Ex. 124-6
——— triads (progression of, round the circle of keys, by successive dominants) . . . . Ex. 120
——— triads (progression of, round the circle of keys, by successive subdominants) . . . . Ex. 122
Modulation by diminished seventh . . . . . 140-4, Ex. 160
——— by dominant seventh round circle of keys . Ex. 144-5
——— by dominant seventh 128-39
——— to augmented fourth above, by dominant (figurated)
  Ex. 155-7
——— to major second above, by dominant (figurated) Ex. 150-1
——— to major third above, by dominant (figurated) . Ex. 156
——— to major third below, by dominant (figurated) . Ex. 153
——— to minor second above, by dominant (figurated) Ex. 147
——— to minor second below, by dominant (figurated) Ex. 152
——— to minor third above, by dominant (figurated) . Ex. 158
——— to minor third below, by dominant (figurated) . Ex. 149
——— to perfect fifth above, by dominant (figurated) . Ex. 148
Modulative agencies (dominant and diminished tetrads as) 127

N.

Notation (aspect of, with ostinato motives) 65
——— (of all accompaniment expression undesirable) . . 70
——— (various aspects of diminished seventh chord, in) . 142
Notes in common between chords (a means of modulation)
  129, 137
——— in common between chords (illustrated) Ex. 146, Ex. 154

O.

Obbligato basses 13
Octaves (prevalent use of, when melody in bass) 41
Orchestral motives in accompaniment 13
——— parts (condensation of, as accompaniment to choral music) 52

Organ character of polyphonic accompaniment 48
——— -point 40
Origin of rhythmic figures 96-8
Ostinato figures (association of different, in the same vocal
  piece) 103
——— figures (association of different in the same vocal
  piece), illustrated . . . . Ex. 118-9
——— figures of accompaniment 93-4, 101, 103
——— motive 65-7
Over use of thumb in left-hand double notes 45

P.

Passing-notes in characteristic figure . . . . 100, Ex. 116
Phrase-chord 6, 21, 24-5, 93*a*
——— -chord (common use of) . . . . Ex. 19
——— -chord illustrated in plain harmony arpeggio and
  tremolo . . . . Ex. 17
——— -chord in association with interspersed symphony Ex. 18
——— (extension of the) 11
Plain harmonisation . . . . 4, 93*a*, Ex. 2
Polyphonic accompaniment . . . . Ex. 10
——— accompaniment with melody as upper part . 50, Ex. 50
Polyphony 12, 48, 93*b*
——— consisting of one part only, against the voice 48, Ex. 48
Positions 118
——— of diminished seventh chord 140
Precision (importance of, in simple passages) 16

Q.

Qualification of the reader 1
Quaver as minimum rhythmic pulsation 7

R.

Regulated and unregulated tremolo 75
——— tremolo . . . . Ex. 88
Repeated chords . . . . 80, 82, 93*d*, Ex. 93-5
——— chords (with association of other features) . . Ex. 96

Rhythm 6, 11, 23
Rhythmic figure . . . . 32, Ex. 29
—— figure in bass (independent) . . . . . . 33, Ex. 30
—— figure in bass (subordinate) . . . . . . 34, Ex. 31
—— figures (formation of simple) . . . . . Ex. 110
—— figures (illustrated) . . . . Ex. 111-3
—— figures of accompaniment . . . . Ex. 90-2
—— pulsation (minimum) . . . . . . 7, 33, Ex. 5
Rhythm (lightness of, as compared with that of notes) . . 79

S.

Sforzando in tremolo 22
Side contact of note-heads in tetrad positions . . 121, 124
Single note preceding double note (considered as a form
   of accompaniment) 74
—— note preceding double note (considered as a form
   of accompaniment, illustrated) . . . . Ex. 87
Six-note semiquaver groups . . . . Ex. 77
Slur (its twofold use) 16
Solo pianoforte music (accompaniments in) 14
——-player and accompanist compared 101, 106
—— practice requisite for cultivation of some features
   of accompaniment 44
Sostenuto accompaniment 6
—— power of piano sometimes exceeded 23
Styles of accompaniment (table of) . . . . Ex. 11
Subdominant 55
Subdominants, successive (progression of triads by) . Ex. 55
Suspensions (use of, in connection with diminished
   seventh) 142
Syncopation 78, 84
—— in chord repetition . . . . Ex. 99

T.

Tabular exposition of styles of accompaniment . . Ex. 11
Tenor of accompaniment (melody in) 44
Tetrad-positions 123-4
——-positions (first inversion) . . . . . . Ex. 135

Tetrad-positions (illustrated)	Ex. 134
———-positions (second inversion)	Ex. 136
———-positions (third inversion)	Ex. 137
——— (side contact of) second in notation, a sign of	Ex. 133
Tetrads (the five illustrated)	Ex. 142
Text (interspersed symphony used in illustration of)	22
"Three against two" in cross-rhythm	85
Third (as representing minor or major triad)	Ex. 129
——— (interval of, as representing triad)	115
Tone (amount required to be gathered from form of accompaniment)	70-1
Tonic and dominant (each two succeeding triads in relation of)	55
Touch (graduations of, required when melody in bass)	41
——— (how to secure uniformity of ostinato motives)	65, 102
——— required for large chords in *pianissimo*	31, Ex. 28
——— required for plainly harmonised accompaniments	29
Transient modulations by chromatics	147
Transposition	111, 116, 124, 127, 152-162, Ex. 171
——— to other key bearing same letter	154
——— to other key, second above or below	157
——— to other key (table of)	Ex. 172
——— to other key, third and fourth above and below	160-1
Tremolo	75
———, a favourite adaptation of the "phrase-chord"	21
——— (lightness of, desirable)	22
Triad progressions extended positions	Ex. 59
——— progressions octave positions	Ex. 57-8
——— progressions by successive dominants	Ex. 52
——— progressions by successive subdominants	Ex. 55
——— (various dispositions of the notes which form the)	118-22, Ex. 131
Trio for manuals and pedal (resemblance to produced by two-part polyphonic accompaniment and voice)	49, Ex. 49
Triplet group (practical application of)	61
——— group (practical application of) with greater sostenuto and chromatic changes	Ex. 64-5
——— group (practical application of) with sostenuto bass	Ex 63

General Index. 231

Triplet group (practical application of) with staccato
    bass) . . . . Ex. 62
——— groups (as the result of dispersion of simple triad) . 60
——— groups (exercise on successive dominants) . . Ex. 60
——— groups (exercise on successive subdominants . Ex. 61

U.

Underchanging note 126, 128
——— note (use of, exemplified in passing round circle
    of keys by dominant seventh) . . . . . . Ex. 144-5
Unison 93*a*
——— accompaniment . . . . Ex. 1
——— accompaniment (common fault in) . . . . Ex. 12
——— accompaniment (harmonically inflected) . . 20, Ex. 16
——— accompaniment (varieties of) . . . . . 17, Ex. 14
——— character imparted to ensemble by melody as bass
    of accompaniment 41
———, Figurations of . . . . 18-9, Ex. 15

V.

Visible aspect of intervals in notation 121-2
Voice (bass of accompaniment in dialogue with) 42
———-part (necessity of reading, with accompaniment) 101
——— (stationary against changeful harmony in accom-
    paniment . . . . 26-7, Ex. 23
——— (supremacy of, when in combination with instru-
    ments) 2
Vulgar treatment of melody as bass of accompaniment . . 41

www.ingramcontent.com/pod-product-compliance
Lightning Source LLC
Chambersburg PA
CBHW010741170426
43193CB00018BA/2911